LIVING WITH HEROES

This book is dedicated to my wife, Ethel, my family and, in particular, to absent friends.

Guy Gibson when a fighter pilot

Living With Heroes

The Story of the Dam Busters

Harry Humphries
Adjutant 617 Squadron 1943–1945

THE ERSKINE PRESS
2003

LIVING WITH HEROES

First published in 2003 by
The Erskine Press, The Old Bakery, Banham, Norwich
Norfolk NR16 2HW

ISBN 1 85297 081 2
British Library Cataloguing-in-Publication Data
A catalogue record of this book is available
from the British Library

Printed and bound in Great Britain by
Antony Rowe Ltd, Chippenham, Wiltshire

Contents

Author's Note

I first started these memoirs way back in the early '50s but they were left unfinished until quite recently. The original pages, now yellowing with age, have been retyped, and added to. It can be claimed, without a doubt, that these memoirs are a 'first' of the 'Dambusters' stories, as they were written as it was lived from my service from 1943 to 1945 as Adjutant of 617 Squadron, firstly under the command of Wing Commander Guy Gibson, VC, DSO, DFC, then Wing Commander Leonard Cheshire, VC, DSO, DFC and finally J. B. 'Willie' Tait, DSO, DFC.

However, approaching the 1950s, I received a letter from Paul Brickhill, already well known because of his book, *The Great Escape*, who asked for access to my diaries. He had been commissioned to write the history of 617 Squadron by Royal Air Force 'top brass'. To be fair, all concerned were completely unaware that I was well advanced with my story. I was however more than a little upset when my efforts looked unlikely to bear any fruit in the face of such formidable opposition. My reply to Brickhill was very negative and, looking back, more than a little petulant.

I have included copies of some of the letters from Paul Brickhill and Leonard Cheshire, the latter entreating his ex-Adjutant to make his material available. I could never oppose the wishes of 'Chesh' and all that I had written was given to Brickhill, and the *Dambusters* story and the film followed. I accepted this situation but retained my material and over the years I wrote many articles for various publications but I never got around to actually finishing the book. But, one after another, *Dam Busters* books came along, all by 'non-participants, and finally a story came that was so incredibly untrue that I decided my story must be finished.

Included here are copies of the original DamRaid operation plans, some interesting memorabilia about the joint UK/Russian operation to sink the battleship, *Tirpitz*, details of the crews who took part in the original raid and finally, the Roll of Honour.

I am greatly indebted to a number of people for their willing help and information. In particular I must thank Alan Bateman, Robert L. Wray, Rick Brand and Derrick Warren. Their assistance was invaluable.

These details – the Roll of Honour, the letters and the plans, are the only records in existence. What we have here is a little piece of history, offered by one 'who was there' on 16th May 1943.

Preface

Many may wonder why, after fifty years, I, as the Founder Adjutant of 617 Squadron have taken all this time to present my version of the Dam Busters. My family, when I have been persuaded to talk of my two years with the Squadron, believe I should tell my story because it is evident that of all the writers who have written about the 617 Squadron, I am the only one who was actually there, living daily with the bomber crews.

Paul Brickhill's *Dam Busters*, which was depicted on film, and Professor John Sweetman's version were two well-researched books, excellent in their own way, but were written by people who were not connected with the Squadron. From its foundation under Wing Commander Guy Gibson until the end of hostilities in 1945 when I was posted to the far Eastern theatre of war, I remained Adjutant. There have been other offerings and 'jumpers on the bandwagon', some were good guesses, and some outrageously incorrect (I must mention *617 Squadron, The Dam Busters at War* by Tom Bennett who was our Navigation Officer, but this was well into the post Dam Raid period, and his is a factual story of that time.) It is probably due more to these 'stories' that I have been convinced, even at this late stage that I should present the words that I typed nearly fifty years ago.

I served under Wing Commander Guy Gibson VC, DSO, DFC; Wing Commander Leonard Cheshire, VC, DSC, DFC (later Lord Cheshire), and Wing Commander J. B. 'Willie' Tait, a quadruple DSO. In my capacity as Squadron Adjutant I had personal contact daily with these war heroes. No other author of the Dam Busters story can claim this honour, so perhaps it is right that I should make my contribution before it is too late. The words I put on paper in the fifties are perhaps lacking in professional expertise but they are honest and true. I thank all those who gave me the tremendous experience of working with them and to them, with deference, I dedicate my story.

Guy Gibson claimed me as his Adjutant in March 1943 and he told me very briefly just what he expected me to do. Just as I was leaving his office, after quite a long discussion, he stopped to make his final remark: 'This squadron will either make history or it will be completely wiped out, Adj.' I looked at him rather hard, I suppose not knowing whether I had heard him correctly, 'I beg your pardon sir,' I said but he was not listening, just poring over a map. How right the little man was. The squadron did make history and was once nearly wiped out but under such great leaders as Wing Commander Gibson, Wing Commander Cheshire and Wing Commander Tait the Squadron gained a name which will ever be great in the records of Bomber Command.

I propose to record this, not because I think I should be a novelist, but because I feel guided by a sense of duty to finish off a story which, I suppose, 'Gibby' started.

I was very fond of the Squadron boys, both air and ground crew, and I had many happy times and many sad times. Joy and tragedy overtook us periodically, sometimes almost in a matter of minutes. As an adjutant I was a 'wingless wonder', non- operational, privileged only to fly when I could squeeze apologetically into an aircraft.

1 THE RAID

It was the evening of 15th May 1943. The comfortable officer's mess at Scampton was, unlike most non-ops nights, crowded with RAF types. They were standing in groups by the large fireplace, some reading in the comfortable armchairs, others draped in fantastic attitudes on chairs, tables and stone cold radiators. The main drink that evening was orangeade and suchlike and we all knew that something was about to happen but didn't know exactly when, if, or why. But anyway, the boys were taking no chances and were keeping off the liquor.

The only person, if one can call a dog a person, taking a drink was the Wingco's dog 'Nigger'. He was an habitual drunkard anyway. As I write this I have thought for the first time that it may be against the principles of the RSPCA to allow a dog to get drunk, but it doesn't matter much anyway because poor old 'Nigger' has been dead and buried for many years. I have always had a strong sense of the dramatic and even though the setting I have described may not appear out of the ordinary to most people it made me tingle with expectancy. I found myself interpreting glances and whispers as something great and significant, and at times I would look at someone who was doing nothing more dramatic than drinking lemonade and wondering how long he had got to live. You get like that as a Bomber Squadron Adjutant: wondering to whom you have to send that terse official telegram: 'We deeply regret to inform you…,' or who's wife will be coming to see you and will they be brave or will they cry. Back in civilian life I often received lectures from my companions in business on the way they suffered during the war, in contrast to the free and easy life that I enjoyed throughout my period of service in the Royal Air Force. I never argue. I have my memories.

On this particular evening I was in the company of an air gunner friend, Flying Officer Gregory, a Scotsman born and bred. Old Greg was a tough proposition, tall, handsome and, like most Scots, very independent. If he liked you, all well and good. If he disliked you, well at least you knew. He was actually kicking over the traces at this particular moment. Greg's wife had been in Lincoln a few days previously and I really think he felt that he needed her in his strung up state. He did not know what he wanted to do. First he wanted to go out in his car and find a drink, then he wanted to play snooker, and then he would talk about bed and

change his mind just as rapidly. So I said 'Come on old lad, let's go for a walk around the mess. It's getting damned hot in here.' He said 'OK Adj. we'll go and see the wee doggie.' Just as we were leaving the anteroom John Hopgood, Gregory's pilot, spotted us and aimed an almost playful kick at his rear gunner's backside, which I am sure would have crippled him if it had landed. When I eventually separated them, with Greg, needless to say, on top by sheer brute force, Hopgood or 'Hoppy' as we knew him, dragged himself painfully to his feet. 'Just as I said,' he complained loudly, 'air gunners are all bloody brawn and no brains.' I hurriedly dragged Gregory away before they really maimed one another. 'Nigger' looked at us through bleary eyes as we left the room. It was a beautiful evening. It was difficult to imagine this as a bomber aerodrome, there for the sole purpose of dealing out death to our enemies.

Harry Humphries before his appointment to 617

The birds were whistling gaily and the crowded flowerbeds around the mess were telling the world that they were ready to burst forth into a profusion of colour at any moment. It all sounds rather poetic. A couple of corpulent officers were gambolling around the tennis court vaguely lashing out at a small white ball. They weren't aircrew. Those boys had other things on their mind. Greg and I walked silently along to the married quarters where we lived in one of those comfortable little houses which had been vacated by families because of the war. When we reached our place, our batman, I forget his name now, but he was a good chap, was standing outside playing with Gregory's dog. She had given birth to a fine litter of pups of very doubtful origin. The Station Commander's spaniel had been blamed for her motherhood, but my bet was that the father was the Alsatian from the garage down the road.

'Good evening gentlemen,' said the batman, who I shall call George, 'can I get you your usual?' Greg rumbled, 'You certainly can lad, with plenty of sugar.'

Our usual was nothing more glamorous than a cup of tea, mashed sometimes as a refresher and sometimes as an antidote for a hangover. This was usually consumed in George's little kitchen over an informal chat about current affairs and general small talk. George loved to show off his art gallery, which consisted of photographs of his conquests prior to his recent marriage. His wife now occupied pride of place. He was so short sighted that I often wondered if he could tell one from the other anyway.

This little man had the most varied vocabulary of expletives that I have ever heard. I found this out by chance when he poured some hot water on his feet one day and I don't think the kettle ever recovered! This particular evening we couldn't get going with our current affairs discussion, George seemed to be uneasy while Greg was miles away, possibly with that soft voiced pretty little wife of his.

According to the best novels there should now be a cold wind blowing through the house and sending a chill down our backs and freezing our hearts, but nothing like that happened. We were just nervy knowing that something was going to happen. The night remained as warm and inviting as it ever was.

Greg was the first to move. 'I think I will go to bed' he said, 'may be working tomorrow'. With that he had gone and little did I know that for Greg it was probably his last cup of tea in that kitchen. In fact it was his last night on earth. As I write, this seems a rather crude way of putting it, but it is, never-the-less, a cold, hard fact. Greg would never again see his wife, and I was to lose a good friend. He wasn't the first or the last, I know, but this little episode is written merely to emphasise the numerous tragedies that happened daily in Bomber Command.

I rose to go. 'Well I'm off back to the mess, George. In case you're in bed when I come back, goodnight.'

'Very good sir,' said George, 'cup of tea at seven'.

'Yes please,' I said, thinking why the hell does he always ask me that stupid question. I always have my tea at seven. Perhaps I was being a bit irritable.

[3]

On my way back I ran into the little man himself, Wing Commander Gibson, who was standing in the road in his shirtsleeves. ' Is that you Adj.?' he said.

'Oh hello sir,' I replied. 'Are you feeling fit?'

'Top of the world, old Humphries,' was the reply. He usually called me that: I was an old man of some 28 summers while he was a juvenile of around 26 years. I cannot remember the Wing Commanders' exact age but I believe his records state his year of birth was 1918. I mention this because most articles and books dealing with this great pilot's career seem to insist that he was twenty-five in 1942 and 1943 and 1944. This all made him quite a Peter Pan, so contrary to entries in all other epistles, I state emphatically that he aged twelve months every year, the same as everyone else. This is all by the way. He stood there on this beautiful summer evening looking as happy and carefree as anyone would after a spot of digging or planting in the garden. He knew so much more than anyone else, too. He knew the type of operation about to be launched at the unsuspecting Germans in the Ruhr, and he knew that the chances of survival were about 50/50, maybe less, and yet he could smile. Not that the Wing Commander always smiled. When he was at his business commanding a bomber squadron he could be ruthless and, while never sparing himself, did not spare others either. Inefficiency he could not or would not tolerate and many that came to our Squadron departed as quickly as they had come.

If I have any criticism it is that he could be most tactless at times. This may have been due to his youth or his tremendous responsibilities, but who am I to judge? There is one incident which stands out in my memory. We had a 'runner' named Turner, a young man who did everything from sweeping offices to mending the CO's autocycle, and one day the Wing Commander rang for him to perform some menial task. This being completed, Turner started to leave the office when the Wing Commander's voice rang out,

'George, I want you.' Turner proceeded on his way unperturbed and again 'George' rang out. Turner still carried on and then a cyclone came charging through my office. It was the Wingco. He caught Turner just as he was entering the orderly room.

'You bloody fool,' bellowed the CO. 'When I call you it's an order, I've a damn good mind to put you on a charge. Take this envelope to "A" Flight Commander.'

He came back through my office mumbling and threatening. I thought, 'ah well, such is life'. About an hour later Turner entered my office.

'Excuse me sir,' he said.

'Well Turner, what is it,' I replied.

'I'm a bit upset. The Wing Commander just rousted me.'

'Well why didn't you stop when he called you,' I said.

He looked rather embarrassed. 'My name isn't George sir, that's why I didn't stop. I thought the CO was calling somebody else.'

Now it was my turn to flounder. 'Oh, very good Turner, I will mention it to the Wing Commander.'

I did mention it to the CO. He looked at me and then very deliberately rang for the 'runner', three rings. In came the wretched Turner.

'Turner,' said the Wingco, 'I understand your name is not George.'

'No sir,' said 'George'.

The Wing Commander jumped up and banged the table, 'If I call you George and you have no further intelligence than to think I am talking to a brick wall, then I am sorry for you.' He frowned ominously and almost whispered, 'Now in future George, you are George, understand George.'

Turner mumbled, 'oh, um, yes sir', and beat a hasty retreat. The Wing Commander looked at me. I was trying very hard to see something interesting out of the window, without success.

'Bloody fool,' he muttered. I didn't answer. I didn't even know whether he meant me or the unfortunate 'runner'.

It is not really a very important incident, insignificant in fact, but our 'Gibby' often did things like that, particularly when he was telephoning. He seemed to think the system was installed purely for his benefit and an engaged number meant to him an inefficient operator. Many an unfortunate WAAF switchboard operator no doubt has recollections of the Wing Commander's voiced opinion of their ability. However, as I said, who am I to judge? For my own part, if he had given me orders to jump in a lake, or any other instructions with such dire consequences, I would probably have done it. Wing Commander Gibson was a superb Commanding Officer, worked like a man inspired and created inspiration in others.

To return to our meeting, very little happened to record, just small talk. Everything he had on his mind he kept to himself.

'What have you been doing with yourself this evening Adj.?' he said.

'Well nothing special sir, the odd drink you know, and a walk around and so to bed I suppose. Anything you want me to do before I turn in?'

'Er, not really old boy, may have plenty of work for you tomorrow though. Oh yes, you can take "Nigger" for a walk for me, I think he has a date with a lamp-post or my carpet.' He laughed, 'Sooner a lamp post I think.'

He whistled and a very sorry looking dog struggled out of the mess door.

'Come on "Nigger",' I said, trying to coax him on to the road. Poor lad couldn't take it and returned to the sanctuary of his master's room.

The CO roared. 'Looks like my carpet after all Adj. Well I'm off to bed, pleasant dreams.'

It just occurred to me that I referred to the Wingco as the 'little man'. This is really an endearing sort of name that we gave him, because tough though he was, he was only a little man; but what a man! I thought I would have another look in the anteroom to see if any of the boys were still about. My first stop was at the bar and the barman was sitting there in solitary splendour. I consumed half a pint of Newark ale and strolled into the anteroom where there were only two other persons, both members of the Station Headquarters. I nodded in their direction, picked up a magazine and began to scan it without the slightest interest in its contents. One became like that in the Services. To read anything more complicated than the newspaper headlines was a strain, to plan for the future was too uncertain really, to be normal wasn't normal. I threw the magazine down after bidding goodnight to the two other officers, and departed to find my bed.

So we come to 16th May 1943. It was to be an exciting and thrill packed day, one I know that I shall remember all my life. Nineteen aircraft were to take off against the enemy. Out of that nineteen only eleven were to return and fifty-three young men were to lose their lives in dealing the greatest ever single blow against the enemy war machine. Three, Pilot Officer Anthony Burcher DFM, Flight Sergeant J. W. Fraser, and Flight Sergeant F. Tees were to languish in prisoner of war camps for three long dreary years. Seventy-seven were to survive this time, but many perished later. This was 'the toll of Bomber Command'.

Breakfast came like any other. Porridge or cereal followed by sausage and potatoes. Then marmalade, and dry toast. No person knew this was the day, 'der tag' as I call it in my diary, and if any individual thought it was they were prepared to ignore the fact. I was in my office early ready for any developments and they began early. The Wing Commander crashed in just after 9.00 am.

'Flying programme Adj.,' he said.

'Training programme sir?' I asked.

'No, um, that is yes to the rest of the Station,' he answered. Seeing the look of bewilderment on my face at this statement he said, 'We are going to war at last but I don't want the world to know about it so do not mention the words "Battle

Order", just make out a night flying programme. All who should know will receive their orders verbally.'

He spent considerable time giving me full details of the nineteen crews, together with the Code Order for the Attack. Then the Station broadcasting system called together all the crews of 617 Squadron.

He said, 'Well I'm off now, Adj. God knows when the flak will die down but I'll try to give you mealtimes and take off details later.' Then he dashed off, hatless, with a bulky red file marked 'Most Secret' under his arm. All through the day preparations proceeded quietly and efficiently. All the major snags were overcome. If they had not have been overcome the praised 'Dam Busters' raid would never have come to pass.

There was another squadron – the 57th – at Scampton. Even though we lived in the same mess, none of the men of 57 Squadron were ever aware that we were operating until 617 Squadron returned to base, and the waters of the Möhne and Eder dams were cascading into the Ruhr valley. The security officer at Scampton, Flight Lieutenant Evans, I believe, did a grand job of work. His job was made easier due to the magnificent co-operation of both the ground and aircrew of the Squadron. Through six weeks of rigid censorship there was not one instance of a breach of security at Scampton. I saw only fleeting glimpses of most of the faces I knew that day. Group Captain J. N. H. Whitworth DSO, DFC, the Station Commander was amongst them. He was one of the best, and under his command Scampton was a very happy and contented Station. He managed to get the best out of all of his men without unduly cracking the whip, a procedure which when adopted is thoroughly disliked by members of the Royal Air Force. Not that the RAF is lacking in discipline. Its record throughout the war contradicts any criticism in that direction.

After I completed all of the preliminary administrative arrangements, the flying programme, the organisation of the aircrew flying rations, plus sundry other paper work jobs, I needed only the times of take off and return from the Wing Commander. I did not ultimately receive them from him direct but through a 'runner' who handed me a sealed envelope addressed to me in the CO's handwriting. It gave take off hours and estimated time of return. I cannot rightly remember the time, but I think that it said take off would be about 2100 hours, and the time of return about 0300 hours. From these times I had to work out such things as the buses to take the aircrews to their planes in good time to complete the preliminary

[7]

crew drills and prevent unnecessary rush and a meal time to allow the boys to catch the buses. In between mealtimes and bus times I had to ensure that flying rations were available, and coffee which the aircrew carried in the aircraft whilst on operations. I had to be available to accept cash, wills, and letters to next of kin, should anyone wish to deposit such articles. Strangely enough, the men who did deposit anything with me always seemed to return to collect it.

Harry Humphries in 1943

From the point a view of the return to base after the operations, arrangements had to be made for transport to collect the crews from their machines to take them from interrogation and then onwards to their mess for the usual eggs and bacon; of course the eggs and bacon had to be arranged. On top of this there were sundry other jobs of work such as issuing Bomber Command Codes, making sure all the dogs were looked after, telling batmen to press uniforms, putting cars into garages and so on, which were passed on to me by the air crew who looked up to the Adjutant as the 'maid of all work'. I'm not grumbling. I loved it. I revelled in it all at that time.

I did have a bit of trouble with the meals on this occasion The WAAF Sergeant in the Officer's mess kitchen, when I told her I wanted full operational flying meals for normal night flying programmes, was adamant that it could not be done. I told her that it was a special occasion, and it was a very arduous flight and also that it had the blessing of the Station Commander. Still, no, she had her orders and she was sticking to them. I stormed and I cajoled and I wheedled but to no avail. Finally I practically had to intimate that it was not really a normal training flight, and let it go at that. She beamed. 'Why didn't you say so in the first place sir, I knew all the time really.' I looked to heaven, cursed all WAAF cooks under my breath, and hastily left the kitchen. Still, the meals had been arranged.

Evening came and all the Squadron personnel, the air crew, the motor transport drivers, the cooks, the mechanics, the armourers, the photographers, had either done their job of work or were standing by ready. It was a beautiful night again, warm and inviting and in the messes the aircrew were making their final preparations. Those not on duty were on the airfield waiting and watching for the take off for this operation which was to make history. In the Officer's mess, there were a lot of strange faces; high ranking Air Force Officers and several studious looking civilians – 'the back room boys' – including the originator of the weapon which breached the dam so successfully. I felt awfully small in the midst of all this activity. I wanted to help everybody to do something, but no help was needed. We had all done our little piece of the jigsaw and we were ready. I went to my office at six pm. And waited

I mention in passing that even in my confidential capacity as Adjutant I still had no idea of the target, or the type of operation, or of anyone else involved except the flying men. I just knew that it was something terrific and I was thrilled to be involved in some small way, even if only to deal with the 'bumf' or paperwork. There was one upsetting incident already mentioned in Guy Gibson's 'Enemy Coast Ahead'. 'Nigger' the only beer-drinking dog I ever knew, and the Wing Commander's closest friend, had been killed by a car. I know personally that the Wing Commander looked on this as a very bad omen, but he brushed this to one side and give us the peculiar order to bury the animal outside his office at 2300 hours. This was duly done, and later a cross was placed on the grave with due ceremony. As far as I know it may still be there outside the big hangar at Scampton.

At last the activity commenced in earnest, the aircrews began to turn up, on bicycles, in battered little cars and on foot. I began to check. Yes, all the buses were ready, the flying rations were OK, the coffee was available and in the distance the Lancasters stood silent, ominous looking, waiting to be unleashed at the enemy.

I decided to have a walk around and a chat to some of the boys. I saw Gregory, again quite cheerful, with his flying kit over one arm. Some of the fellows were lying around on the grass surrounded by Mae Wests, parachute harnesses and other items of flying equipment. Henry Maudsley, OC 'A' Flight, was in earnest conversation with his crew; the other Flight Commander was strangely enough tidying up his office. Les Munro, a New Zealand Flt Lieutenant, was sprawled in a chair reading an ancient copy of *T.M.*, an RAF Magazine. They were all there, those who were to survive and the others – fifty-three men with but a short time to live; grand young men, from Canada, Australia, New Zealand and our own native land. It seems so dreadful that they cannot be sitting here with me where I am writing this story surrounded by flowers and apple trees in my own garden. Perhaps if they were here with the knowledge of the still wavering international situation it would make them sigh. Instead I sigh for them.

It was getting near zero hour. The stocky figure of Wing Commander Gibson could be seen descending from his car. I call it a car but it was so loaded with humanity at times that it resembled a Lincolnshire bus. He walked around among the boys, chatting, always smiling and if he was worried he certainly didn't show it. I thought I had better say something to him before he took off and I walked over but before I could say a word, Trevor-Roper, his rear gunner, butted in.

'Hello short arse,' he greeted.

I flushed a little. Trev. always annoyed me, but I couldn't do much about it. Every time I retaliated he just held me in one hand, a very big hand, and threatened to spank me with the other. I gave him a glance which should have withered him completely, but he just smiled right across his face. When Trevor-Roper smiled he just grinned from ear to ear and resembled a very sinister stage villain.

I did manage to catch the eye of the Wing Commander however, and I said, 'Anything you want me to do sir?'

'Always on the spot Adj.,' he replied. 'I don't think there is anything at the moment; oh yes, there is though. Plenty of beer in the mess when we return. We'll be having a party'. He looked thoughtful and added, 'I hope'. With that he turned to his crew and said 'Well chaps, my watch says time to go. Cheerio Adj., and don't forget the beer.'

His departure was the signal for the general exodus. The buses began to fill rapidly and trundle around the perimeter track to the waiting aircraft. Soon there were only a few stragglers left. Dave Shannon's crew were looking for their pilot. He was seen to be strolling nonchalantly from the locker room, apparently without a care in the world. Flt Lieutenant David John Shannon, DFC was a cool customer. He had completed one tour of operations, been awarded his decoration and had volunteered for this job, and he still had to celebrate his 21st birthday.

He was greeted by a variety of remarks by his crew: 'Pull your finger out David, don't let us worry you', and 'have you cleaned your teeth?' David grinned, and walked elegantly into the crew bus; then they were gone and all was quiet.

Flight Sergeant Powell, the squadron disciplinarian, and Sergeant Heveron, the orderly room Sergeant, were standing talking to a group of ground staff airmen and a few WAAF, waiting to see their favourite pilot take off, were leaning on the railings. The final diversion was caused by Flt Lieutenant McCarthy, DFC, of the

Royal Canadian Air Force. The silence was disturbed by a roar resembling a clap of thunder and we suddenly saw Mac emerging and charging towards the flight offices like a runaway tank. Flight Sergeant Powell, ever alert, met him before he could reach us.

'What's the matter sir.'

McCarthy spluttered. 'My bloody aircraft is u/s, I've got to take the spare. There's no compass deviation card. Where are those lazy, idle, incompetent compass adjusters?' We calmed him while many willing people searched for the missing compass card. Mac was in a mess. He stood six feet one inch and weighed about 15 stone. The excitement and exertion had really disturbed his equanimity. His shirt was wringing wet and he gulped in great breaths of air. His huge hands were clenching and unclenching spasmodically.

'Calm down old boy,' I said. 'You'll make it.'

Flight Sergeant Powell came running towards us with the all-important card in his hand. 'Here you are sir,' he said as the sound of aircraft engines starting up could be heard.

'Listen now,' said Mac, rushing off with a card in one hand and his parachute in the other. Alas, he was holding the ripcord instead of the proper handle, and as he ran towards the Lancaster yards of parachute silk streamed out from behind him. He didn't stop, but merely flung it to the ground like a discarded dishcloth. Within five minutes of him entering the aircraft his engines were started, and I remember thinking that he may make a mess of the whole thing, taking off in such a state. But Mac was not that sort of chap. He went and he came back and earned a DSO for his pains.

Now the great machines began to lumber around the airfield to the take off points. Lancasters always reminded me of ducks. They seemed to waddle and in spite of the fact that I had seen many take offs, I always found each one interesting and rarely missed the chance to see them. That night I didn't go to the marshalling point where one could get a grandstand view and give a final wave to each aircraft before the pilot released the brakes to launch his machine along the runway. I don't know why I didn't go; maybe I felt a little strung up, or something like that. Anyway I watched each Lancaster become airborne from the window of my office but I did go outside to see all the boys roaring away into the fast approaching twilight, and that was a great thrill because they were flying at less than 150 feet from the ground. I just stood and gaped, hardly able to realise the significance of it all. A voice disturbed me. I shook myself out of the coma which had overtaken me so rapidly. Flt Sergeant Powell stood against me with a voice full of emotion.

'Grand night sir,' he said, 'I do hope they finish the job. They have worked so hard.'

'Yes, yes, so do I, Flight. Well we'll know within a few hours,' and I added, 'are you going to stay up for their return?'

'You bet. Are you coming down to the flight sir?'

'I must see the Squadron back on their first op. mustn't I?' I said and I tried to sound casual.

'I suppose so, sir.' He drew himself up. 'In case you need me, sir, I'll be in my office.'

He saluted, correctly as always, and turned around and walked away. A great little man, Powell. He was the father of two families – his own wife and children and all the airmen of the Squadron, the latter presenting the greater problem but in both cases he was an excellent parent. He had started out as a carpenter in civilian life, but eventually this had proved too 'hum drum'. He chose the Royal Air Force as a career, had now served several years and my only regret is that I had never been able to exercise enough influence to obtain authority for his promotion to Warrant Officer.

Lancaster – City of Lincoln

The Crews

A FLIGHT

G   Wing Commander G. P. Gibson, DSO, DFC
     Sgt John Pulford
     FO Harlo 'Terry' Taerum
     FltLt R. E. G. 'Bob' Hutchinson, DFC
     PO F. M. 'Spam' Spafford
     PO George A. Deering
     FltLt R. A. D. Trevor-Roper, DFM
(Deering had been commissioned and Taerum promoted to FO before the flight and without their knowledge)
Attacked Möhne Dam then proceeded to Eder Dam to direct operations. Returned to base.

A   Squadron Leader H. Melvyn 'Dinghy' Young, DFC & bar
     Sgt D. T. Horsfall
     FltSgt C. W. Roberts
     Sgt L. W. Nichols
     FO V. S. MacCausland, RCAF
     Sgt G. A. Yeo
     Sgt W. Ibbotson
Attacked Möhne Dam then proceeded to Eder Dam as deputy commander. Shot down returning to base. No survivors.

B   Flight Lieutenant W. 'Bill' Astell, DFC
     Sgt J Kinnear
     PO F. A . Wile, RCAF
     WO2 A. Garshowitz, RCAF
     FO D. Hopkinson
     FltSgt F.A . Garbas, RCAF
     Sgt R. Bolitho
Crashed over Holland on inward flight. No survivors.

J   Squadron Leader David J. Maltby, DFC

        Sgt W. Hatton
        Sgt V. Nicholson
        Sgt Anthony J. Stone
        PO Jack Fort
        FltSgt V. Hill
        Sgt H. T. Simmonds

Attacked Möhne Dam. Returned to base.

L   Flight Lieutenant David J. Shannon, DFC, RAAF

        Sgt R. J. Henderson
        PO Danny R. Walker, DFC
        FO Brian Goodale, DFC
        FltSgt Len J. Sumpter
        Sgt B. Jagger
        PO Jack Buckley

Attacked Eder Dam. Returned to base.

E   Flight Lieutenant Robert N. G. Barlow, DFC, RAAF

        PO S. L. Whillis
        FO P. S. Burgess
        FO C. R. Williams, DFC, RAAF
        PO A. Gillespie, DFM
        FO H. S. Glinz, RCAF
        Sgt J. R. G. Liddell

Shot down on inward flight. Bomb recovered by Germans. No survivors.

H   Pilot Officer Geoff Rice

        Sgt E. C. Smith
        FO R. MacFarlane
        Sgt C. B. Gowrie
        FltSgt J. E. Thrasher
        Sgt T. W. Maynard
        Sgt S. Burns

Hit sea and aborted flight. Bomb torn away. No attack. Returned to base.

C   Pilot Officer Warner Ottley, DFC, RCAF

        Sgt R. Marsden
        FO J. K. Barrett, DFC

Sgt J. Guterman, DFM
FltSgt T. B. Johnston
Sgt H. J. Strange
FltSgt Freddie Tees
Shot down before reaching target. Only Freddie Tees survived.

F   Flight Sergeant Ken W. Brown, RCAF
Sgt H. Basil Feneron
Sgt D. P. Heal
Sgt H. J. Hewstone
Sgt S. Oancia
Sgt D. Allatson
FltSgt G. S. McDonald
Bombed Sorpe Dam. Returned to base.

K   Pilot Officer Vernon W. Byers, RCAF
Sgt A. J. Taylor
FO J. H. Warner
Sgt J. Wilkinson
PO A. N. Whittaker
Sgt C. McA. Jarvie
Sgt J. McDowell, RCAF
Shot down on inward flight. No survivors.

B FLIGHT

Z   Squadron Leader Henry E. Maudslay, DFC
Sgt J. Marriott, DFM
FO R. A. Urquhart, DFC, RCAF
WO2 A. P. Cottam, RCAF
PO M. J. D. Fuller
PO W. J. Tytherleigh, DFC
Sgt N. R. Burrows
Attacked Eder Dam. Bomb struck parapet. Shot down. No survivors.

M   Squadron Leader John V. Hopgood, DFC & bar
Sgt C. Brennan
FO K. Earnshaw
Sgt J. W. Minchin

PO J. W. Fraser, RCAF
PO G. H. F. G. Gregory, DFM
PO Anthony F. Burcher, DFM, RAAF
Hit by enemy fire but bombed Möhne Dam before being shot down. Only rear gunner Fraser and bomb aimer Burcher survived.

P   Flight Lieutenant Harold B. 'Micky' Martin, DFC
PO Ivan Whittaker
FltLt Jack F. Leggo, DFC
FO Len Chambers
FltLt R. C. 'Bob' Hay, DFC, RAAF
PO B. 'Toby' Foxlee, DFM, RAAF
FltSgt Tammy D. Simpson, RAAF
Attacked Möhne Dam. Returned to base.

W   Flight Lieutenant J. Les Munro
Sgt F. E. Appleby
FO F. G. Rumbles
Sgt Percy E. Pigeon
Sgt J. H. Clay
Sgt Howarth
FltSgt H. A. Weeks
Aircraft intercom damaged. No attack. Returned to base.

T   Flight Lieutenant Joe McCarthy
Sgt W. Radcliffe
PO D. A. MacLean
Sgt L. Eaton
Sgt G. L. Johnson
Sgt R. Batson
FO D. Rodger
(MacLean had been commissioned before the operation, without his knowledge)
Attacked Sorpe Dam. Returned to base.

S   Pilot Officer Lewis J.Burpee, DFM, RCAF
Sgt G. Pegler
Sgt T. Jaye
PO L. G. Weller

WO2 S. J. L. Arthur, RCAF
Sgt W. C. A. Long
WO2 J. G. Brady, RCAF

(Arthur had been promoted to WO2 before the operation, without his knowledge)

Shot down on inward flight. No survivors.

N Flight Lieutenant Les G. Knight
    Sgt R. E. Grayston
    FO H. Sidney Hobday
    PO R. G. T. 'Bob' Kellow, RAAF
    FO E. C. Johnson
    Sgt F. E. Sutherland
    Sgt H. E. O'Brien

(Kellow had been commissioned before the operation, without his knowledge)

Attacked Eder Dam. Returned to base.

O Flight Sergeant W. C. 'Bill' Townsend
    Sgt D. J. D. Powell
    PO C. L. Howard
    FltSgt G. A. Chambers
    Sgt C. E. Franklin
    Sgt D. E. Webb
    Sgt R. Wilkinson

Attacked Ennepe Dam. Returned to base.

Y Flight Sergeant Cyril T. Anderson
    Sgt R. C. Paterson
    Sgt J. P. Nugent
    Sgt W. D. Bickle
    Sgt G. J. Green
    Sgt E. Ewan
    Sgt A. W. Buck

(Anderson had been commissioned before the operation, without his knowledge)

Mechanical problems. No attack. Returned to base.

Two crews did not fly on the dam raids because of illness. They were:

Pilot Officer W. G. Divall
    Sgt D. W. Warwick
    Sgt J. S. Simpson
    Sgt R. C. McArthur
    Sgt Murray
    Sgt E. C. A. Balke
    Sgt A. A. Williams

Flight Sergeant Harold S. Wilson
    Sgt T. W. Johnson
    FO J. A. Rodger
    Sgt L Mieyette
    PO S. H. Coles
    Sgt T. H. Payne
    Sgt E. Hornby

Both these crews were later killed in action on the ill-fated Dortmund Ems Canal raid in September 1943.

No. 617 SQUADRON.

No.	A/C.	Captain.	F/Engr.	Navigator.
1.	G.	W/CDR. GIBSON.	SGT. PULFORD.	F/O. TAERUL
2.	M.	F/LT. HOPGOOD.	SGT. BRENNAN.	F/O. EARNSHAW.
3.	P.	F/LT. MARTIN.	P/O. WHITTAKER.	F/LT. LEGGO.
4.	A.	S/LDR. YOUNG.	SGT. HORSFALL.	SGT. ROBERTS.
5.	J.	F/LT. MALTBY.	SGT. HATTON.	SGT. NICHOLSON.
6.	L.	F/LT. SHANNON.	SGT. HENDERSON.	F/O. WALKER.
7.	Z.	S/LDR. MAUDSLAY.	SGT. MARRIOTT.	F/O. URQUHART.
8.	B.	F/LT. ASTELL.	SGT. KINNEAR.	F/O. WILE.
9.	N.	P/O. KNIGHT.	SGT. GRAYSTON.	F/O. HOBDAY.
10.	W.	F/LT. MUNRO.	SGT. APPLEBY.	F/O. RUMBLES.
11.	K.	F/LT. McCARTHY.	SGT. RATCLIFFE.	F/SGT. McLEAN.
12.	H.	P/O. RICE.	SGT. SMITH.	F/O. MacFARLANE.
13.	K.	SGT. BYERS.	SGT. TAYLOR.	P/O. WARNER.
14.	E.	F/LT. BARLOW.	SGT. WILLIS.	F/O. BURGESS.
15.	C.	P/O. OTTLEY.	SGT. MARSDEN.	F/O. BARRETT.
16.	S.	P/O. BURPEE.	SGT. PEGLER.	SGT. JAYE.
17.	O.	F/SGT. TOWNSEND.	SGT. POWELL.	P/O. HOWARD.
18.	F.	F/SGT. BROWN.	SGT. FENERON.	SGT. HEAL.
19.	Y.	F/SGT. ANDERSON.	SGT. PATERSON.	SGT. NUGENT.

617 Squadron DamRaid Battle Order

The Raid

ING PROGRAMME 16.5.43.

ptr.	A/Bomber.	Front Gunner.	Rear Gunner.
JTCHISON.	P/O. SPAFFORD.	F/SGT. DEERING.	F/LT. TREVOR-ROPER.
NCHIN.	F/SGT. FRASER.	P/O. GREGORY.	P/O. BURCHER.
AMBERS.	F/LT. HAY.	P/O. FOXLEE.	F/SGT. SIMPSON.
CHOLS.	F/O. MacCAUSLAND.	SGT. YEO.	SGT. IBBOTSON.
ONE.	P/O. FORT.	SGT. HILL.	SGT. SIMMONDS.
OODALE.	F/SGT. SUTTER.	SGT. JAGGER.	P/O. BUCKLEY
OTTAM.	P/O. FULLER.	F/O. TYTHERLEIGH	SGT. BURROWS.
RSHOWITZ.	F/O. HOPKINSON.	SGT. GARBAS.	SGT. BOLITHO.
KELLOW.	F/O. JOHNSON.	SGT. SUTHERLAND.	SGT. O'BRIEN.
GLON.	SGT. CLAY.	SGT. HOWARTH.	F/SGT. WEEKS.
ATON.	SGT. JOHNSON.	SGT. BATSON.	F/O. RODGER.
ARIE.	F/SGT. THRASHER	SGT. MAYNARD.	SGT. BURNS.
LKINSON.	SGT. WHITAKER.	SGT. JARVIE.	SGT. McDOWELL.
LLIAMS.	SGT. GILLESPIE.	F/O. GLINZ.	SGT. LIDDELL.
THERMAN.	F/SGT. JOHNSON.	SGT. TEES.	SGT. STRANGE.
LLER.	SGT. ARTHUR.	SGT. LONG.	F/SGT. BRADY.
CHALMERS.	SGT. FRANKLIN.	SGT. WEBB.	SGT. WILKINSON.
WSTONE.	SGT. OANCIA.	SGT. ALLATSON.	F/SGT. McDONALD.
CKLE.	SGT. GREEN.	SGT. EWAN.	SGT. BUCK.

[21]

COPY   TOP SECRET
                                   M O S T   S E C R E T
                                        COPY NO......

NO. 5 GROUP OPERATION ORDER NO. B.976

APPENDIX 'A' - ROUTES AND TIMINGS

APPENDIX 'B' - SIGNALS PROCEDURE FOR
              TARGET DIVERSIONS, ETC.

APPENDIX 'C' - LIGHT AND MOON TABLES.

INFORMATION.

Ceneral.

1.   The inhabitants and industry of the Ruhr rely to a very large extent on the
enormously costly water barrage dams in the Ruhr District.   Destruction of TARGET X
alone would bring about a serious shortage of water for drinking purposes and
industrial supplies.   This shortage might not be immediately apparent but would
certainly take effect in the course of a few months.   The additional destruction of
one or more of the five major dams in the Ruhr Area would greatly increase the effect
and hasten the resulting shortage.   TARGET Z is next in importance.

2.   A substantial amount of damage would be done, and considerable local flooding
would be caused immediately consequent on the breach of TARGET X.   In fact it might
well cause havoc in the Ruhr valley.   There would be a large loss of cooling water
for the large thermal plants.

3.   In the Weser District the destruction of the TARGET Y would seriously hamper
transport in the Mittelland Canal and in the Weser, and would probably lead to an
almost complete cessation of the great volume of traffic now using these waterways.

4.   The reservoirs usually reach their maximum capacity in May or June, after which
the level slowly falls.

Enemy Defences.

5.   (a) TARGET X.

        There are three subjects on the crest of this dam which may each be a light
        A.A. gun.   A light 3-gun A.A. position is situated below and to the N. of
        the dam with a possible searchlight position nearby.   A double line boom
        with timber spreaders is floating on the main reservoir at 100 to 300 feet
        from the dam.   No other A.A. position or defence installation is known.

      (b) TARGETS Y and Z

        Information about the defences of these two dams will be given when P.R.U.
        sorties have covered these areas.   (Information has now been issued).

      (c) The last resort targets are unlikely to be defended.

INTENTION

6.   To breach the following dams in order of priority as listed :-

      (a) TARGET 'X'   (GO 939)
      (b) TARGET 'Y'   (GO 934)
      (c) TARGET 'Z'   (GO 960)
      (d) Last Resort Targets:-
            (i)   TARGET 'D'   (GO 938)
            (ii)   TARGET 'E'   (GO 935)
            (iii) TARGET 'F'   (GO 933)

                                              /EXECUTION ....

[22]

EXECUTION   TOP   SECRET.

Code Name.

7.   This operation will be known by a code name which will be issued separately.

Date of Attack.

8.   The operation is to take place on the first suitable date after 15th May, 1943.

Effort.

9.   Twenty Special Lancasters from 617 Squadron.

Outline Plan.

10.   The twenty special Lancasters of 617 Squadron are to fly from base to target area and return in moonlight at low level by the routes given in APPENDIX 'A'.   The Squadron is to be divided into three main waves, viz:-

(a)   1st Wave.   Is to consist of three sections, spaced at ten minute intervals, each section consisting of three aircraft.   They are to take the Southern route to the target area and attack Target X.   The attack is to be continued until the Dam has been clearly breached.   It is estimated that this might require three effective attacks.   When this has been achieved the leader is to divert the remainder of this wave to Target Y, where similar tactics are to be followed.   Should both X and Y be breached any remaining aircraft of this wave are to attack Z.

(b)   2nd Wave. - Is to consist of five aircraft manned by the specially trained crews who are to take the Northern route to the target, but are to cross the enemy coast at the same time as the leading section of the 1st wave. This 2nd wave are to attack Target Z.

(c)   3rd Wave.   Is to consist of the remaining aircraft and is to form an airborne reserve under the control of Group H.Q.   They are to take the Southern route to the target but their time of take-off is to be such that they may be recalled before crossing the enemy coast if the 1st and 2nd waves have breached all the targets.

Recall will probably not be possible unless the first section of the 1st Wave are at POSITION 51°51' N., 03°00'E. by Civil Twilight (EVENING) + 30 minutes and the 3rd Wave must be at this position 2 hours 30 minutes later.   Orders will be passed to aircraft on the Special Group frequency if possible before they reach the enemy coast instructing them which target they are to attack.   Failing receipt of this message aircraft are to proceed to X, Y and finally last resort targets in that order, attacking any which are not breached.   Officer Commanding, R.A.F. Station, Scampton, is to arrange for individual aircraft to be detailed to specific last resort targets.

Detailed Plan.

11.   The 1st Wave is to take off in three sections each of three aircraft and fly to the target at low level by the route given in Appendix 'A'.   Sections are to be spaced at intervals of ten minutes and are to fly in open formation.   Height is not to exceed 1,500 feet over England.   On leaving the English Coast aircraft are to descend to low level and set their altimeters to 60 feet using the Spotlight Altimeters for calibration.   The QFF at various stages of the route is to be carefully noted Aircraft are to remain at low level for the Flight to the target and on the return journey at least until crossing a point 03°00'E.

- 3 -   TOP SECRET

as low as possible both going in and coming out even if it is necessary to climb a littl]
later for map reading.

13.   On arriving at a point 10 miles from the target the leader of each section is
to climb to about 1,000 feet.   On seeing this all other aircraft are to listen out
on V.H.F.   Each aircraft is to call the leader of the Wave on V.H.F. on arriving
at the target.   Spinning of the special store is to be started ten minutes before
each aircraft attacks.   The leader is to attack first and is then to control the
attacks on TARGETS X and Y by all the other aircraft of the 1st Wave using the
Signals procedure given in APPENDIX 'B'.

14.   Number 2 of the leading section of the 1st Wave is to act as deputy leader
for the whole of the 1st Wave during the attack on TARGET X.   Should the leader fall
out No. 2 of the leading section is to take over leadership, and No. 3 deputy leadership, for the attack of TARGET X.   For the attack of TARGET Y Number 4 is to take
over deputy leadership, or if No.1 is absent he is to take over leadership, in which
event No. 7 is to be the deputy leader.   All other aircraft are to return by Route 1,
the second three by Route 2 and the last three aircraft of this wave by Route 3.

15.   The direction of attack of TARGET X is to be at right angles to the length of
the target.   The general direction of attack is, therefore, to be S.E. to N.W.
Aircraft are not to be diverted to TARGET Y until TARGET X has been breached.   If
TARGET X is breached, up to two additional aircraft may be used, at the discretion
of the leader, to widen the breach in TARGET X providing at least three aircraft
are diverted to attack TARGET Y.

16.   When TARGET X is seen to be breached beyond all possible doubt the leader is to
divert the remainder of the first Wave to TARGET Y by W/T and V.H.F. where similar
tactics are to be used for the attack of this target.   The general direction of attack
of TARGET Y is to be from N.W. to S.E.   If target Y is seen to be breached beyond all
possible doubt all remaining aircraft of the 1st Wave are to be diverted by the leader
to attack TARGET Z independently using the same tactics as the 2nd wave.

18.   For the attacks of both Targets X and Y the special range finder is to be used,
the height of attack is to be 60 feet and the ground speed 220 m.p.h.

19.   The 2nd Wave is to take off and fly to Target Z at low level by the Northern
Route given in Appendix 'A'.   Aircraft are to cross the enemy coast in close concentration, but not in formation, at the same time, although at a different point, as the
leading section of the 1st Wave.   Aircraft on this Wave will be controlled on the
alternative V.H.F. channel.   The special stores are not to be spun for the attack of
Target Z.   Aircraft are to attack this target from N.W. to S.E. parallel to the length
of the dam and are to aim to hit the water just short of the centre point of the dam
about 15 to 20 feet out from the edge of the water.   Attacks are to be made from the
lowest practicable height at a speed of 180 m.p.h. I.A.S.   Aircraft are to return to
base independently.   First two aircraft by Route 1; second two aircraft by Route 2
and the last by Route 3.

20.   The 3rd Wave is to consist of the remaining aircraft and is to form an airborne
reserve under the control of Group Headquarters.   They are to fly to Target X in close
concentration, but not in formation, at low level by the Southern route given in
Appendix 'A'.   These aircraft are to be at Position 51°52' N., 03° 00'E.   2 hours
30 minutes after the leading section of the 1st Wave have crossed this point on their
outward route to the target.   Orders for the 3rd Wave will be passed to all aircraft
on the special Group frequency, if possible before they reach the enemy coast,
instructing them which target they are to attack.   Failing receipt of this message
aircraft are to proceed to X, Y and, finally, last resort targets in that order
attacking any which are not breached.   The 3rd Wave are to use tactics of attack

/similar to those ...

TOP SECRET

similar to those used by the 1st Wave when attacking Targets X and Y except that attacks on last resort targets are to be made independently. After attacking, aircraft are to return to base independently at low level by any of the three return routes given in Appendix 'A'. Aircraft attacking early should take Route 1; the next aircraft Route 2 and the last Route 3.

Method of Attack.

21.   Aircraft are to use the method of attack already practiced. The pilot being responsible for line, the Navigator for height, the Air Bomber for range and the Flight Engineer for speed.

22.   The interval between attacking aircraft is to be not less than three minutes all targets.

23.   On all targets except Target Z each aircraft is to fire a red verey cartridge immediately over the dam during the attack. Aircraft attacking Target Z are each to fire a red verey cartridge as they release their special store.

24.   All aircraft are to fly left hand circuits in each target area keeping as low as possible when waiting their turn to attack.

Time of Attack.

25.   The time of attack of each target by each wave is not important to within a few minutes. The time of crossing the enemy coast is, however, all important. ZERO HOUR, which will be given in the executive order, is, therefore, to be the time at which the first section of the 1st wave are to be at POSITION 51°52'N., 03°00'E. on the outward route to the target. This time will probably be Civil Twilight (EVENING) + 30 minutes. At this time aircraft of the 2nd Wave should be about Position 53°19'N., 04°00'E.

Routes.

26.   As in Appendix 'A'.

Diversions.

27.   The whole essence of this operation is surprise, and to avoid bringing enemy defences to an unnecessary degree of alertness, diversionary attacks must be carefull timed. H.Q. B.C. will be asked to arrange the maximum possible diversionary attacks so that the first enemy R.D.F. or other warning of the diversionary attacks occurs 20 minutes after the leading section of the 1st wave crosses the enemy coast. No diversionary attacks should be despatched which would cross the enemy coast for a period of one hour preceding the 3rd Wave. 15 minutes after the 3rd wave cross the enemy coast further diversionary attacks should be made at maximum strength and should continue, if possible until the 3rd wave are clear of enemy territory on the return journey. Diversionary attacks below 2,000 ft. should not be made in the area bounded by the points (51°00'N., 03°20'E), (51°20'N., 06°30'E), (51°00'N., 10°00'E.)., 52°00'N., 09°00'E.). (53°20'N., 06°00'E.). H.Q. B.C. will also be asked to arrange suitable weather reconnaissance to report in particular on the visibility in the target area at least in sufficient time to recall the Lancasters before they cross the enemy coast if the weather is unsuitable.

Armament.

28..   (a) Bomb Load. - Each Lancaster is to carry one special modified store (UPKEEP)

        (b) Ammunition.- All guns to be loaded with 100 night tracer (G VI).

Fuel.

29.   The Lancasters may take off at a maximum all up weight of 63,000 lbs. at .14 boost. As the modified store now weighs about 9,000 lbs. 1750 gallons of petrol can be carried.

Navigation.

- 5 - TOP SECRET

switched on at Z - 20 minutes and to remain on for the whole of the operation. This should assist in making an accurate landfall on the enemy coast at the correct time.

31.   The route is to be carefully studied before flight and the outstanding features, obstructions and pinpoints noted, particularly water pinpoints. E.T.A.'s at each are to be carefully calculated and if any pinpoint is not found on E.T.A. a search is to be made before proceeding to the next pinpoint.   Aircraft may climb to 500 feet shortly before reaching each pinpoint if necessary to help map reading.

32.   The maximum use is to be made of the Air Position Indicators.

Synchronisation of Watches.

33.   All watches are to be synchronised with B.B.C. time before take off on the day of the operation.

Secrecy.

34.   Secrecy is VITAL.   Knowledge of this operation is to be confined to the Station Commander, O.C. 617 Squadron and his two Flight Commanders until receipt of the EXECUTIVE signal.   After crews are briefed they are to be impressed with the need for the utmost secrecy because of the possibility that the operation may be postponed should weather reconaissance prove the weather to be unsuitable.

Reports.

35.   Each aircraft as soon as possible after it has attacked is to report by W/T on the normal Group operational frequency in accordance with APPENDIX 'B'.

Special Devices.

36.   MANDREL and TINSEL are not fitted.

37.   IFF is NOT to be used on the outward journey but normal procedure is to be followed on the homeward flight.   Any aircraft returning early is NOT to use IFF except after Z + 30 minutes for the 1st and 2nd Waves and after Z + 3 hours for the 3rd Wave.

Nickels.

38.   Nickels are not to be dropped.

INTERCOMMUNICATION.

Wireless Silence.

39.   Strict W/T and R/T silence is to be maintained until after Z + 30 minutes for the 1st and 2nd Waves and after Z + 3 hours for the 3rd Wave.   Any aircraft returning early is NOT to break W/T or R/T silence and is NOT to identify on MF/DF except after Z + 30 minutes for the 1st and 2nd Waves and after Z + 3 hours for the 3rd Wave.   Aircraft returning before that time are to cross the English Coast at 1,500 feet at the point of exit and proceed direct to base or the nearest suitable airfield.   Otherwise normal operational signals procedure is to be used except as modified by Appendix 'B'.

MF/DF Section.

40.   Section D is to be used if required in accordance with Paragraph 39.

Executive Order.

41.   The executive order for the operation will be given by EXECUTIVE followed by the code word allotted, the date on which the operation is to take place and the time of Zero Hour in British Double Summer Time.

/42.

[26]

- 6 -

TOP SECRET

42.   ACKNOWLEDGE BY TELEPRINTER.

(Sgd.) H.V. SATTERLY G/C
Senior Air Staff Officer,
No.   5   Group,
Royal   Air   Force.

Ref:- 5G/101/54/Air.
Date:- 16th May, 1943.

DISTRIBUTION

External.	Copy No.
Group Captain J. N. H. Whitworth, DSO., DFC.	1 and 2.
Headquarters, Bomber Command. (Deputy C.-in-C. personally, or in his absence, Group Captain N.W.D. Marwood-Elton, D.F.C.).	3, 4 and 5.

Internal.

Action Copy (Ops. II).	6 .)
	)Not to be
C.S.O.	7)issued until
	)after
File.	8)despatch
	)of
Spares.	9, 10, 11,)Executive
	and 12.)Signal.

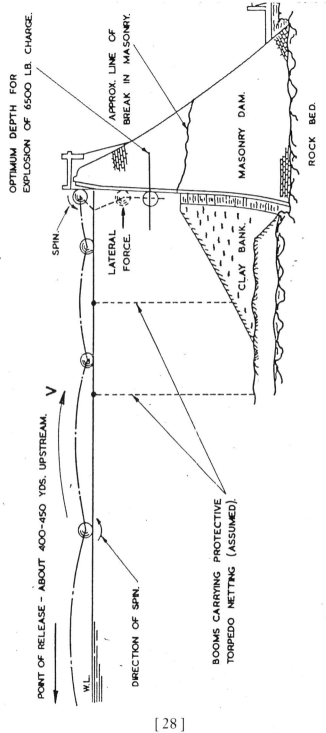

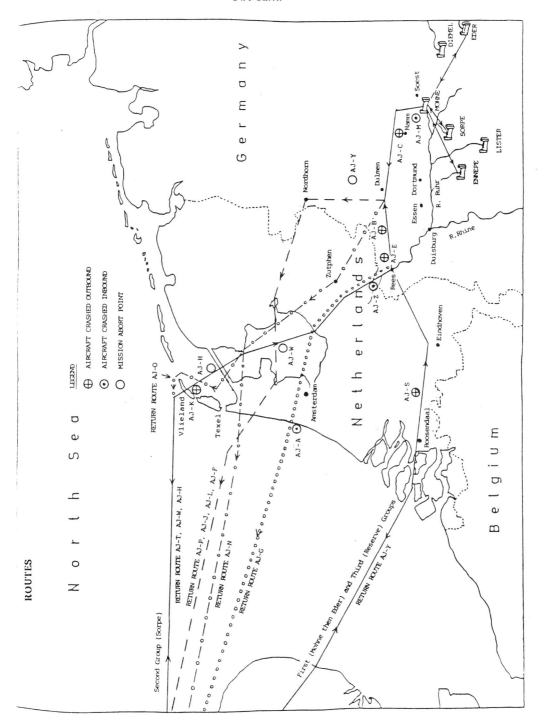

ROUTES

2 WAITING

I strolled back slowly to the mess, thinking hard of my own particular friends taking part in the operation. There was Flt Lieutenant R. E. G. 'Bob' Hutchison DFC, who flew as a wireless operator with the Wing Commander. We had worked on the stage in RAF shows. I couldn't bear to think that he might not return, though he did on this particular occasion. I thought of Twink, his girlfriend in Boston. Bob was one of the few bomber boys I knew who did not drink. He either went to Boston or read a book when off duty. He had a stronger will power than most of us. Then I thought of Flying Officer Jack Buckley. He was the ace drinker of the Squadron and yet I have seen him shoot ten out of ten clay pigeons on the morning after the night before; an amazing character, and funnily enough he was also a marvellous golfer.

Other names flitted across my mind; the CO of course, Les Munro, Dave Maltby, Bill Astell, Dinghy Young, Les Knight. What would tomorrow mean to them? For some it never came.

I eventually arrived in the mess anteroom. The back room boys were still with us; Flt Lieutenant Caple, the Engineer Officer, and Doc Watson the Armament Officer, who was already honoured with the MBE. And one other person I haven't yet mentioned, though she was just as much one of us as any of the others – Section Officer Fay Gillon, a WAAF Intelligence Officer. She was attached to 617 Squadron for duty and I know that she loved her work. Her main worry was that she knew the attachment would eventually come to an end, and when this occurred she would no longer have any connection with the Squadron but would proceed back to her post at Station Headquarters. We liked her around. She was pretty and in spite of all the written things about beautiful, glamorous WAAFs littering up Air Force stations, they were not so numerous!

I sat against Fay. She was a little pink around the cheeks.

'You look excited,' I said.

'Oh I am excited,' she replied, 'isn't it too marvellous Humphy, no Squadron has ever done a job like this.'

I started; so she knew the target. I felt a bit annoyed. Here was I, Adjutant to the Squadron not knowing that 'vital secret' and yet a slip of a girl was evidently in the confidence of the selected few. Of course common sense indicated that as an intelligence officer she would have to know, or so I told myself.

'I hate to disillusion you Fay but I don't know the target.'

Now it was her turn to start. 'You don't?'

'No,' I admitted, rather annoyed at having to do so.

'Well, I, um, you know I can't say anything don't you?' She said this apologetically.

'Of course Fay, perhaps a little later when your conscience is clear,' I said. I changed the subject and offered her a drink. I think we both needed one then. Here we were safe in one piece on the ground, getting all het up, just like a couple of hens worrying about their chicks.

The time passed very slowly. Occasionally the silence in the anteroom would be broken by a stifled cough, or whispered conversations. Why the hell people had to whisper I don't know, but then I found myself doing it every time I addressed Fay Gillon or anyone else. I kept nodding off and suddenly I imagined I heard the sound of an aeroplane. I must have been dreaming. No, it wasn't a dream. The drone came nearer. Everyone in the room was listening.

I heard Caple say, 'An early return.' He came across to me: 'Coming over Adj. to see who it is?'

By now I was fully awake and I followed Caple out of the mess. We arrived on the airfield just in time to see a huge machine land. There was a roar as the pilot throttled back, then he was running safely along the ground. We found the machine at its dispersal point, easily visible with landing lights blazing and much to our amazement we could also see shadowy figures running away from the machine. Caple stopped one of these shadows – an airman who was puffing and panting and not at all happy.

'What's the matter?' Caple snapped.

'Flt Lieutenant Munro sir.' The man's mouth opened and shut again.

'Well?' said Caple.

'He has just landed with his bomb still on, and I think it's going to drop off.'

With that, officers or no officers, the airman left at top speed.

'Oh, we had better go and see,' said Caple.

I gulped, and crossed my fingers. The Lancaster looked very sinister to me now. We managed to get quite close and could see quite plainly the bulky outline of the missile underneath the aircraft. Caple evidently thought it better to seek expert advice, and he swung his van round and put his foot flat on the boards and within a few seconds we were back in the mess. With equal speed Caple found Doc Watson the Armament Officer. After hearing the story the Doc was unperturbed,

'I'll just nip across and see what all the flap is about,' he said, and added, 'funny things, bombs.'

'Can it go up at any moment Doc?' I gasped.

'Maybe,' he said laconically, 'but I bet my lads have solved the problem already, and if they haven't, then you'd better duck.'

We heard later that all was well. Doc's men had the situation under control and the men we had seen running were not the armourers. They had been there all the time and in fact as soon as the machine reached the dispersal point they were examining the bomb. Funny job, armourer. One minute here, then bang, no more. It used to make my flesh creep when I saw them sitting astride big bombs, which used to be a favourite photograph in those air force days.

Eventually the pilot of the aircraft came into the mess. It was Flt Lieutenant Munro the New Zealander. He had been 'shot up' over enemy territory; the aircraft intercommunication having being severed. He was 'hopping mad' with his bad luck, so much so, that his meal of eggs and bacon hardly interested him. Poor Les was even more depressed when after the raid the surviving pilots were awarded the DSO. He would never consider the point of view that he could well have been one of the unlucky ones who failed to return.

Another machine, piloted by Flying Officer Rice, also had to return from the operation. Jeff Rice was also furious at not having completed the trip, but a trifle more subdued than Munro. He had perhaps more reason to be, for he had brushed the North Sea when flying low. His missile had been torn from the Lancaster and exploded in the sea only a matter of yards away from the tail of the plane. Apart from the horrible thought that he was nearly blown to eternity, Rice also had on his mind his terrific struggle with the huge bomber, trying to prevent it diving straight beneath the waves. Both of these pilots now joined forces with the rest of us waiting in the anteroom.

It was fast approaching the time for the return of the bomber force. Someone had the bright idea of switching on the wireless and tuning into the short wave, for the purpose of contacting our returning aircraft. It worked sometimes, and sometimes the reception was completely unintelligible. On this occasion it actually did function quite well, for as soon as we heard the first machine circling the aerodrome, we picked up quite clearly the pilot's request to land. I am not sure now but I think it was Squadron Leader Maltby. I began to get excited, even more so when I got a glimpse of that almost fictitious character, 'Bomber' Harris, the C-in-C Bomber Command.

Bombs away! – the attack on the Gnome-Rhône factory at Limoges

I remember clearly hearing 'G' for George, and 'G' for Gibson asking for permission to come in. The 'little man' was back! On hearing that I left the mess for the flight offices to greet some of the returning heroes, and also to get first hand information of all that had happened. The first person I saw, stowing away flying kit, was Dave Maltby.

'How was it Dave?' I queried.

'A terrific show Adj., absolutely terrific. I have never seen anything like it in all my life,' he said, then, quite bluntly, 'Hoppy's bought it.'

'Bought it, when?' I asked.

'Shot down over the target, and I am afraid we have lost several others too,' he answered. He pushed his Mae West viciously into his locker. 'Some didn't even get there and I am sure "Dinghy" Young got into trouble, and maybe Henry Maudsley.' He turned and gave me his usual broad grin. 'We pranged it though, Adj. oh boy did we prang it! Water, water everywhere. "Gibby" was everywhere. How the hell the Jerry gunners missed him I don't know.' He added, 'Did you bury "Nigger" for the Wingco?'

I started, 'I, um….to tell you the truth, Dave, I don't know. Why do you ask anyway?'

'Oh it was just worrying Gibby, I know. It just struck me that superstition means nothing anyway, even though I always take this hat with me.' 'This hat' was David's field service or 'fore and aft'. It was a filthy thing, covered in oil and grease but he would not be separated from that hat, even on parade. 'Well, see you later over a beer,' he said and shouted to the rest of his crew, 'so long sprogs, thanks for coming.'

Squadron Leader Maltby addressed his crew as 'sprogs' or 'rookies' for he was the only operational experienced member of the crew, but this night his boys had gained their spurs. Jock Fort, his bomber aimer, had dropped his missile dead on the correct spot. It was his second trip!

After they had left I began to search frantically for evidence of the burial. I had left orders with Corporal Munro that the dog should be buried outside the CO's office, but the ensuing tension had driven it right out of my mind. Munro had not let me down. There was the freshly turned mound outside the Wing Commander's office. The RAF non-commissioned officers were like our London policemen, just wonderful!

I saw more of the crews in, and even though they were in high spirits they confirmed Squadron Leader Maltby's remarks. We had taken a beating as regards casualties. I decided to walk over to the watch office, the flying control tower. My worst possible estimation was insignificant compared with the shock I received. Eight blanks on the blackboard. It was hard to accept. SqnLdr Young, SqnLdr Maudsley, FltLt Astell, FltLt Hopgood, FltLt Barlow, PO Byers, PO Burpee and PO Ottley and all crews, all missing. Two early returns. That left only nine aircraft of the attacking force which had actually come back.

I returned to the mess in a daze. I had to send fifty-six telegrams to next-of-kin. Fifty-six letters to write regretting………….. Eight messages to the Air Ministry, followed by eight circumstantial reports.

After the dam raids a competition was held for a design for a squadron badge and several ideas were shown to George VI and Queen Elizabeth when they visited Scampton. They picked the one shown opposite but its original inscription was *Après nous le déluge*. The inscription was considered somewhat irresponsible by the *Chester Herald* and it was amended to *Après moi le déluge* but this was also turned down until it was pointed out that the design had been personally chosen by the King and the Royal Prerogative should not be challenged. The design was approved.

FROM

J. D. HEATON-ARMSTRONG

CHESTER HERALD

COLLEGE OF ARMS

QUEEN VICTORIA STREET

E. C.

Telephone: CITY 3300.

Telegrams: "ARMSTRONG, LONDON".

25. 8. 43.

NO 617 SQUADRON, ROYAL AIR FORCE

       This Unit wishes to incor-

porate in its Badge a broken dam,

indicative of its successful attack

on enemy dams in May 1943.

       The Motto may be translated as:

AFTER ME THE DELUGE.

CHESTER HERALD.
I.R.A.F.B.

Approved
George R.I

SQUADRON
ROYAL AIR FORCE
617 617
APRES MOI LE DELUGE

J.B. Tait

J.B. Skeeton-Armstrong
Chester Herald
and Inspector of Royal
Air Force Badges.

College of Arms,
March, 1944.

3   'IT IS WITH DEEP REGRET...'

My previous job had been that of collecting personal effects of deceased and missing aircrew. It was now dark and I was glad it was dark. I think I had tears in my eyes and I didn't want anyone to see them.

The scene in the mess anteroom when I walked in was one to be remembered. All the boys were there in flying boots and roll collar sweaters. Some had a mug of beer in each hand. A terrific celebration was in process. I spotted the Wingco and I almost ran up and shook him by the hand.

'Grand effort sir, I understand that you busted a couple of dams.'

'We did Humph, what's the latest news of the latecomers?'

'Eight missing sir,' and I told him the names.

'Humph, bad show.' He was downcast for a moment, then brightened visibly. 'Still we've done as much damage as a thousand-bomber raid. Perhaps shortened the war, so Bomber Harris says. I understand that Churchill is pleased with the result.' He changed the subject, 'A beer Adj.?'

I couldn't refuse, and tried hard to join in their well-earned celebration. The dawn brightened into day, and still the party went on. I could hardly keep my eyes open, yet these lads drank away as though they had just finished a good night's sleep. The only thing that contradicted this was the number of red rimmed eyes to be seen peering into full beer mugs. I had consumed a fair amount of beer but realised it was time for me to go about my duty. I told the Wing Commander that I would go down to the office immediately after breakfast, and asked pertinently if he would be there.

'Have you been up all night Adj.?' he queried.

'Well...yes sir,' I answered, 'but I'm OK.'

'You will stay in bed until lunchtime then and that's an order!'

'Yes sir,' I replied, though I meant to disobey that order, and I did.

There were fifty-six families throughout Britain and the Empire who wanted news of their loved ones, and I, unfortunately, had to send that news. I washed, shaved and finished breakfast as quickly as possible. I managed to escape from the mess without any of the boys trying to pour beer down my throat and my last recollection was of several stubble-chinned, bleary-eyed aircrew types, croaking out dirty songs about the Germans around the mess piano.

When I arrived in the office it would not have surprised me to find all the staff missing because of the celebration in the messes, but no, the old guard were there – FltSgt Powell, Cpl Munro and Sergeant Heveron, plus our small staff. I greeted both the senior NCOs who stood waiting for me to start the day's unpleasant task. We talked together in low voices for some time, until I realised it was time for action.

'Well, Sergeant Heveron, the first job I suppose is the telegrams to the next-of-kin,' I said.

'That's right sir,' he replied.

'Will you prepare them all please, and you, Flight Sergeant Powell, what about the personal effects of all the chaps missing?'

'The billets are all locked sir, and I'm meeting the Committee of Adjustment Officer outside Station Headquarters at 10.00 am,' Powell answered.

'Very well, I don't suppose I shall see much of you today?' I replied.

'No sir, I'm afraid you won't.'

So the day started. I felt frightfully tired and depressed with it all, but it had to be done. We all worked hard until lunchtime when I called a halt. All the telegrams had been duly despatched, as had reports to the Air Ministry. In the Officer's Mess at lunch it was quiet. All the officers taking lunch, that is those of 57 Squadron and Station Headquarters, were talking about the previous night's great raid. The one o'clock news poured forth details to a thrilled world, and through all this I felt like a wet dishcloth.

Immediately after the meal I went back to the office to carry on with the casualty procedure undisturbed. Heveron also returned early, and we continued. The Wing Commander came in happy and smiling at about half past two. He provided the straw to break the camel's back.

'Spot of news for you, Adj.,' he said.

'Yes sir?'

'The Air Officer Commanding is coming down tomorrow to congratulate the boys, and I hear he is going to give everyone leave, including the ground crews,' he said.

'What about…?' I began to say.

'What about you, and the orderly room, Adj.?' he anticipated my question. 'I'm afraid you and I and the clerks will have to stay, we have work to do.'

I really knew that before he told me, but the thought of the entire Squadron going on leave drove me deeper into my fit of depression. It meant so much extra work on top of our present troubles. We had nearly 900 men in all, and each wanted a ration card, a railway warrant and a leave pass. They had to be made out and I had to sign them all – two thousand seven hundred pieces of paper, and the same number of signatures. This didn't end it, for all the names had to be repeated again in Personnel Occurrence Reports, to make sure that we did not draw rations twice, and to obtain ration money and leave pay. There are sundry other fiddling jobs connected with leave, but these are fairly tedious and uninteresting.

I tried to smile at the Wing Commander but I am afraid it must have been a rather sickly effort. 'Ah well sir, the penalty of being a pen pusher.'

'Come into my office Adj., will you?' said the Wingco, 'and we'll map out our working programme.'

I was with him for some considerable time and gradually we evolved our master plan for dealing with the amount of work in hand. The first thing was to complete as much as possible on this day, and tomorrow, after the AOC's address, we would follow on with the remainder of the casualty procedure, including all the letters to the next-of-kin. After that there was another big job of work: the citations for decorations for all of those who the CO considered had earned them on this epic dam raid. There was always plenty to do.

There will always be a lot of criticism levelled at the British system adopted for the recommendation for honours and awards, but it is as fair as it can be. It is just not possible for everyone to get on those lists. The value of those decorations would be negligible.

Needless to say all was done as planned; the casualty procedure, the leave and the recommendations. Subsequently the list of awards for the dam raid was published, and was as follows:

Victoria Cross	One
Distinguished Service Order	Five
Distinguished Flying Cross	Fourteen
Conspicuous Gallantry Medal	Two
Distinguished Flying Medal	Eleven

A total of thirty-three awards to one unit, for one operation. I am not positive but I do not think that this has ever been known in the history of any of the three fighting Services. When one thinks that this Squadron had been formed for just over six weeks, it is all the more amazing. Yet it clearly emphasises the calibre of

Gibson and his men. 617 Squadron had already carved a niche in the annals of Bomber Command. How rapidly the Wing Commander's prophecy was becoming fact! I was also Mentioned in Dispatches for my own small contribution to the dam raid – not like a medal but I was delighted and proud of the recognition for services rendered.

It was now all over and peace reigned at Scampton. The hangars were silent and the Lancasters moored at their dispersal points were waiting for the next job of work. The Ruhr squelched in the mud caused by the operation against the Möhne and Eder dams, while all over Britain the men who had helped to execute this major disaster, as far as the Germans were concerned, were taking a few days well-earned rest.

I just collapsed like a pricked balloon, but at the same time made sure that the first milestone in the history of 617 Squadron was duly recorded in the official history of the unit.

4 TO THE PALACE

For the remainder of May and half of June, 617 did very little but fly on extensive fly-ing training programmes during the day. Apparently none of the 'big chiefs' of Bomber Command had planned anything further for the boys yet. I say this for the training was rather aimless; sometimes low-level dummy attacks, sometimes high-level practice bombing on the local range at Wainfleet sands. Through the lack of operational activity by 617 Squadron there were many 'incidents' in the local pubs, through tactless remarks by rival squadron aircrew. The name 'One-op' Squadron was one of the favourite jibes. In actual fact, one bright spirit of 617 wrote a song all about this, and many a time it was sung around mess pianos. On the whole the majority of the 'incidents' failed to assume major proportions, and were really nothing but healthy inter-squadron rivalry. All aircrew chaps really thought they were members of the Royal Air Force 'ace' Squadron, a good sign of our high morale. There was one important occurrence – on 27th May King George and Queen Elizabeth visited the base to congratulate Guy Gibson and his crews. This was a great honour for the squadron.

Many parties were held in our favourite Lincoln haunts. A small fortune must have crossed the bar counters, and possibly a new record high in hangovers was achieved. Lincoln taxi drivers did sterling work in coaxing belligerent Air Force types into cabs, at all hours of the night, sometimes at the risk of a punch on the nose. Ladies of dubious character tried hard to win the boys over, but generally their wiles were totally inadequate, or their success short lived.

The main event came on 22nd June when all those awarded for their part in the 'Dam Raid' received news of their summons to Buckingham Palace. This was of course a great event and it was decided to organise a mass visit to the metropolis for the occasion. I was asked to organise a special train. Our friends, the RTOs, co-operated very well and fixed us up without much trouble. The station Motor Transport Officer promised a special bus for the journey to and from the LNER

The undermentioned Officers and Airmen have reserved accommodation on the train travelling from Lincoln to Kings X on Monday 21.6.43., and returning on Wednesday 23.6.43.

PARTY GUESTS.

W/Cdr. Gibson V.C., D.S.O., D.F.C.,
S/Ldr. Maltby D.S.O., D.F.C.,
F/O. Johnson D.F.C.,
F/O. Chambers. D.F.C.,
F/Lt. Leggo. D.F.C.,
Sgt. Nicholson. D.F.M.,
P/O. Howard. D.F.C.,
Sgt. Pulford. D.F.M.,
Sgt. Oancia. D.F.M.,
F. Fort. D.F.C.,
F/Lt. Trevor-Roper. D.F.C., D.F.M.,
F/Lt. McCarthy. D.S.O. D.F.C.,
P/O. McLean. D.F.M.,
F/O. Hobday. D.F.C.,
F/Lt. Hay. D.F.C.,
P/O. Deering. D.F.C.,
P/O. Spafford. D.F.C., D.F.M.,
P/O. Foxlee. D.F.M.,
P/O. Brown. C.G.M.,
F/Lt. Wilson.
F/Sgt. Powell.
F/Sgt. Sansom.
Sgt. Heveron.
Sgt. Furze.
Sgt. Elliott.
Sgt. Mins.
Sgt. Chambers.
Sgt. Cammack.
Cpl. Hocker.
F/L. Caple.
F/O. Hodgson.
P/O. Watson. M.B.E.,
F/L. Munro. D.F.C.,
Sgt. Ballard.
F/L. Humphries.

PERSONNEL ATTENDING INVESTITURE BUT NOT ATTENDING PARTY.

F/Sgt. Chalmers. D.F.M.
F/L. Shannon D.S.O. D.F.C.,
F/Sgt. Simpson. D.F.M.,
P/O. Townsend. C.G.M. D.F.M.,
Sgt. Wilkinson D.F.M.,
Sgt. Heal. D.F.M.,
P/O. Knight. D.S.O.
S/O. Gillon.
A.S.O. Fowler.
Sgt. Hewstone.
Sgt. Feneron.

PARTY GUESTS NOT TRAVELLING BY SPECIAL COACH.

F/L. Martin D.S.O. D.F.C.,
F/Sgt. Sumpter. D.F.M.,
P/O. Tearum D.F.C.,
W/O. Taylor.

DETAILS AS FOLLOWS.

TRAVELLING.

Monday 21.6.43. Coach depart Guard Room 13.15 hours. Train departs Lincoln 14.21 hours Change Grantham, arriving Kings X 18.02.

Wednesday, 23.6.43. Train leaves Kings X for Lincoln 13.25 hours. Change Grantham, arriving Lincoln 16.57 hours. Bus back to camp.

ACCOMMODATION.

All personnel are to arrange their own accommodation.

INVESTITURE.

Tuesday 22.6.43. Buckingham Palace 10.15 hours. Party. Tuesday 22.6.43. 19.30 hours. Hungaria Restaurant, Regent Street.

Will all concerned please initial against their names.

station. The manufacturers of the Lancaster aircraft, Messrs A. V. Roe, put the finishing touches to our plans by promising a special party in London in the evening, following the investiture. Many famous people were to be there. In connection with this visit I had to conduct my first briefing of aircrew. I paraded all those going to London in the crew room and I started on a rather quavering note. But once in my stride, and liking the sound of my own voice, I waxed eloquent on the details of train and bus times, and hotel accommodation in London which would cater for those who wished to invite wives and sweethearts. After numerous questions on various details, train tickets were issued, and lists of names checked to ensure correct train booking. We were all set for Buckingham Palace!

The great day duly arrived. We were to proceed without Wing Commander Gibson who we would meet in London. A tremendous party spirit prevailed. In the Officer's mess liquor stocks for the train journey were being purchased by all and sundry, and a fair amount was being consumed at the bar prior to the arrival of the bus. It was a rather comical sight seeing RAF officers waddling out to the bus, with full raincoat pockets. Most of them tried to look nonchalant, but the clink of bottles made it difficult to preserve an attitude of dignity. Some did not even try to hide their intentions, and came out in pairs carrying whole cases of beer! I took a roll call before I dare allow the bus to leave for Lincoln station. I wanted to make sure, most of all, that there were no vacancies in the ranks at the Palace!

The railway officials were very kind when the sudden deluge of Air Force blue struck the station. They even pretended not to notice the cases of beer. The Railway Transport Office was represented by a rather young pilot officer who, unfortunately for him, decided to be officious. He should have sensed the party spirit. He happened to be wearing 'Volunteer Reserve' brass badges in his lapels. The Air Ministry had ruled these out and most of us now had neat little holes to indicate where they had been worn. Two or three of the boys closed in, much to his discomfort. Squadron Leader Maltby started the ball rolling. He toyed with the unfortunate RTO's lapel. 'You shouldn't be wearing these you know,' he smiled broadly.

'N' no sir, I suppose not,' stuttered the Pilot Officer.

'Then we shall have to remove them,' said Dave, with a wink. 'Shan't we chaps?' Before the RTO could move he was seized, and, 'hey presto', he too had two holes in his lapels. Maltby held the two VRs in his huge hand for a moment, and then made his decision. 'You won't be needing these, old boy,' he beamed, 'and may I add you're lucky it's not your trousers.' He threw the badges on to the railway line.

I will say that the RTO took the whole incident in good part. He wouldn't want the badges anyway. From then on he did all his business with me. I was just about his weight, and of course, as Adjutant, I had to set an example, whether I liked it or not. He must have felt relieved however when I was able to tell him that all our party were present and on the train. The Group Public Relations Officer turned up at the last minute. He wanted a story. The whistle had blown, and the train was actually leaving the station as I shouted details. I didn't really tell him very much, but he managed to make a story out of it. Journalists have terrific imaginations.

The screw tops began to come off beer bottles and the party started. When we arrived at Grantham strangely enough we still had a full contingent. Usually on occasions like this someone tries to jump out of a carriage window for a bet! We did have quite a bit of fun on the station. Our carriages had to be shunted on to the London train. Jock Fort and one or two others decided they would like to drive the train. We eventually found them streaked in grime, but very happy, in the driver's cabin. One of the lads was endeavouring to oil the engine, but only succeeded in oiling his best blue uniform!

This time it was not so easy to get them all together. At train departure time, some were in the buffet, some in the toilet, and others had just disappeared. When the train drew out I had a quick check and much to my relief we were still one hundred per cent present. I decided that from now on I would let matters take their own course, otherwise I would finish up a nervous wreck.

The 'gang' had now split into two camps. The quieter and more stable folk, including the married men with wives, occupied half of the accommodation. The rest had started pontoon schools and crap games. I alternated between both. I would have a spell with some of the chaps and their ladies, just to keep myself out of trouble, then I would pop into one of the 'gambling dens', play a couple of hands and sink a quick beer.

After a while the cards seemed to lose their charm, or else some of the lads had lost all their money – I don't know which – and I realised this was the danger period. Plenty of drink had been consumed, and there were wicked glints in many eyes. Poor old Brian Goodale, Dave Shannon's wireless operator, was chosen as subject matter. At this particular time I was talking to the two WAAF officers in our company when suddenly an apparition appeared in the carriage doorway. It was Brian, without his trousers. He had been 'debagged' by the pontoon school. He stood there, weaving a little, with rather a puzzled look on his face.

'Losht my trousers,' he mumbled. 'Very awkward, c….can't go to Buckingham Palashh without my pants, can I?'

The two WAAF looked at me in mute appeal. I had to do something. The tail of his shirt prevented him from being totally indecent, but you could never tell what these fellows might do! I took him down the corridor and shoved him, not too daintily, into the toilet.

'Stay there and wait a minute,' I said. Now I had a rather difficult task to perform. Either I succeeded in getting his trousers back, or I lost mine too. I hoped it wouldn't be the latter. I pushed my way into the carriage where I knew the ceremony had taken place. The wicked gleams were still there. I sighed, hoping for the best. I could see Trevor-Roper there. He would just love to remove my pants! I tried to be offhand.

'Excuse me chaps, have any of you by any chance seen Goodale's trousers?' A roar of laughter greeted the question.

'Why, has he lost them, Adj.?' questioned Dave Maltby innocently.

'You know he has,' I said. 'Now look chaps, I'm not trying to be funny, but he has just walked into a compartment and stood in front of a couple of ladies – like that!' They roared at this until tears streamed down their faces. Jock Fort gasped, 'Quite well made, isn't he?' Another shriek of laughter from all and sundry. I was getting nowhere.

'I think it's frightfully funny too,' I said, 'but you wouldn't think so if it happened to be your lady friends, now would you?' The crisis had passed.

'No, come to think of it I wouldn't,' said Dave Maltby. He pulled a pair of RAF blue trousers from underneath the seat. They were crumpled and covered in cigarette ash. Dave dusted them in a lazy sort of way and tossed them in my direction. 'Thanks,' I said, 'I'll make sure he puts them on.'

'Have a Scotch before you go Adj.,' said Trevor-Roper, fumbling in a suitcase. I didn't really feel like one but thought I had better accept. He handed me the top of a vacuum flask, half full of neat whisky.

'Go on shorty, let's see you knock that back,' he said. I gulped, my prestige was at stake. Taking a deep breath I took the contents of the cup at one swallow. I nearly went through the roof of the carriage. My throat burned away at the sudden contact with the raw spirit, my head swam and tears came to my eyes as I gasped for breath.

'I'm proud of you, Adj.,' said Trevor-Roper. 'Like another?'

Unable to speak, I left the carriage hurriedly, in search of Goodale who should still be in the toilet. He was – and fast asleep, snoring very loudly. I could only think how lucky it was that he hadn't locked himself in. Brian didn't present a very beautiful picture at that particular moment. His mouth gaped open. I shouted, 'Wake up

Brian, we shall soon be in London!' He stirred and mumbled, 'Masser, masser.' One bleary eye opened. He must have been dreaming about his trousers, for as soon as he caught sight of them draped over my arm, he became quite wide awake.

'Ah, so you've found my trousers. Good. Help me put them on Adj. Pleashe…' The ensuing struggle must have resembled an all-in wrestling match. Every time he stood up and raised one leg to his trousers he collapsed with a resounding thud to the lavatory seat. After a nightmare five minutes, he stood there, decent at last, but what a mess! His best trousers were no longer best and most definitely had a date with the nearest cleaner. (To ease any doubts I can confirm that our hero did get to the Palace and looking very, very immaculate.)

That fortunately was the last incident of any real significance. After I had parked Brian in the corner of a compartment, I wandered down the corridor, to seek peace for myself. I noticed one of the chaps leaning out of a compartment window, and thought he was just getting a breath of fresh air. After hearing the peculiar sounds he was making, I realised that he wasn't feeling too good. After that stiff Scotch, neither was I! However, I made my goal and sank into a seat with a sigh, hoping for peace for the rest of the journey to London.

We arrived at King's Cross at approximately six o' clock in the evening. The party then began to split into groups. I was with Trevor-Roper, Joe McCarthy, Jock Fort, Toby Foxlee and Les Munro. I would have been just as safe teaming up with a cage of lions!

No hotel accommodation had been booked. However we were quite optimistic and, in the company of the daughter of a famous wireless comedian, we headed for the Savoy Hotel. It wasn't easy to obtain accommodation in London, as we found out at the Savoy reception counter. However, our lady companion fixed it for us. We were given two rooms, or two suites should I say. Les Munro and I took one, and the rest the other. We had no plans for the evening so after a wash and brush up we gathered in the larger suite and held council. Of course RAF types can't hold a council of war without a drink so we ordered a couple of rounds while we made up our minds. At the finish I was to accompany Toby Foxlee, Joe McCarthy and Les Munro in a round of the town. What a night it was!

I don't even know to this day where I went. I only know that I kept getting in and out of taxis, and meeting dozens of people I had never seen in my life before. I am afraid that I must also reluctantly admit that I was getting rather high. I only know that it was one of the most terrific parties I had ever attended. I suppose I 'shot a line or two' that night. I wouldn't be surprised if I didn't tell someone that I took part in the raid!

It wasn't until the early hours of the morning that we arrived back at the hotel. I am sure that we made sufficient noise to waken the dead, but one or two tactful members of the hotel staff managed to make us realise the necessity for quiet. Making not too soft 'Ssh's' we tiptoed and weaved in the direction of our rooms. Eventually we stopped outside the larger suite.

'Come inside and have a drink chaps,' said Trevor-Roper. 'The party hasn't begun yet.'

I would have preferred to clamber into bed, but knew the futility of objection. So in we went. In the Savoy one had only to press a button and a 'genie' appeared. So we pressed all the buttons and 'hey presto' in came a little man asking us for orders. Needless to say it was a round of beers. After this had been repeated several times heads were beginning to nod, and eyelids droop. Gallantly, Joe McCarthy tried to wake up the party by stripping off, and performing a dance, clad in nothing more modest than a huge bath towel. He lost it several times, and each time he dropped it we all smacked his backside hard. Joe became a trifle fed up with this and, after waving a dignified goodbye with the towel, left to find sleep. This was the signal for the general break up, and I managed to make my room without further incident. I dropped into bed, dog-tired, and must have been fast asleep within seconds.

With the morning came the inevitable hangover. I opened my eyes warily, but it was no use. The ceiling came down and hit me. With a groan I turned over, and tried to go to sleep again. Les Munro appeared in the bathroom doorway.

'Come on,' he said, 'the Investiture starts at 10.15.'

After a few moments deliberation, I clambered dizzily from the bed.

'I don't know why you don't feel like me Les, you should do. You drank plenty last night.'

'New Zealand boy, Adj., we can take it,' he replied easily, but his looks belied the facts. I don't think he felt so good either!

We left for Buckingham Palace just before ten o' clock. I eventually found myself in a queue with Munro, waiting with mothers, fathers, wives and sweethearts of those boys going to collect 'gongs'. When we eventually entered the large auditorium used for Investitures, it was very much like entering a church. Instead of the organ, there was an orchestra playing light music. We were given a seat quite close to the dais. I felt very much out of place in the serious atmosphere. My head felt awful, and in fact I thought I must have looked like something the cat dragged in.

If I looked anything like I felt there must have been a very close resemblance. However, I didn't create any undue interest, so I must have passed muster.

I waited patiently for the arrival of His Majesty the King. All those to be honoured were now lined up, and in the lead was our own CO, Wing Commander Guy Penrose Gibson, and behind him the remainder of 617 Squadron. I believe this is the first and the last time in the history of Investitures that one of His Majesty's fighting forces has been decorated altogether. In any case I am sure that it is the one and only occasion when a single Royal Air Force unit has been in the lead for this distinguished event. There was a rustle at the back of the dais. The band struck up with the National Anthem. Much to my amazement, not the King but our gracious Queen Elizabeth appeared. This again was an unprecedented event. With a smile Her Majesty signified her readiness to begin her arduous task. When I say 'arduous task' it is not merely being polite. The Queen stood there for nearly three hours, never once flagging or failing to give each recipient of a decoration a ready smile and a few words of congratulation.

Wing Commander Gibson was first. Proudly he marched up to receive his Victoria Cross. I wanted to applaud, but this was not permissible. Instead, I tried hard to swallow a huge lump which appeared as if by magic in my throat. 'Gibby'

At Buckingham Palace
(l to r) Len Sumpter, Terry Taerum, Jack Buckley, 'Spam' Spafford, Trevor-Roper, Dave Maltby, Johnny Johnson, Mick Martin, Dudley Heal, Guy Gibson, 'Hobby' Hopday, Dave Shannon, 'Toby' Foxlee, Joe McCarthy, Steve Oancia, Jock Fort, unknown, Len Chambers, Doug Webb, 'Jock' Chalmers

beamed all over his face as he chatted with the Queen. Les Munro, who was sitting next to me, seemed expressionless. I know he was thinking, 'I should be up there to. If it hadn't have been for an unlucky squirt of flack…'. Poor Les Munro. However, he later appeared at the Palace – twice. Once for the DSO and once for the DFC, so he made up for lost time, and unlike a lot of others, he lived.

One by one the remaining thirty-two men of 617 Squadron filed by and duly received their awards. I felt proud of them all. There were many shining eyes in the audience, the eyes of those watching their own particular hero receive his Award of Merit. Soon, all our boys had gone. To me the Investiture was now over. I don't mean this with any disrespect to the others filing up to receive their medals and Orders. It is like attending a school prize distribution. Once your child has received his or her prize, interest flags, but you have to see it through. Maybe a lot of people who have attended Investitures throughout will disagree with me. After the ceremony was over, I made my way into the bright sunshine. It was the usual hustle and bustle of press photographers, eagerly seeking out leading personalities for their news-hungry editors. Guy Gibson and Eve, his wife, had to face a veritable battery of cameras. The boys were photographed walking with Gibson, standing with Gibson, chatting with Gibson, and so on.

The Canadians were photographed, and the New Zealanders, and the Australians, and they posed according to the whims and fancies of the 'news-hounds'. It made me think how nice it would be to be a hero, and I wondered what it would be like. I'll never know unless I save someone from drowning, or stop a runaway horse, which is very unlikely. I don't swim all that well and I don't particularly like horses!

All this however had to come to an end. The Wing Commander and his wife suddenly disappeared, and the name of their destination was whispered through our ranks. The serene atmosphere of Buckingham Palace was to be left behind, and another party was about to begin. We scrambled into the nearest taxi-cab and went in search of the boss. He was eventually tracked down in a well-known London bar, surrounded by admirers. We joined in with great gusto and soon the party was in full swing. The great and mighty rubbed shoulders with the unknown, but everyone was happy.

Toby Foxlee created a diversion, by trying to climb over the bar. He wanted to serve beer to the customers, and the barman objected. They were very good-natured about it all but each time Toby managed to get one foot on the counter he was removed. This roused the Australian fighting blood in Toby. He backed away

The Australian contingent
(l to r) Les Knight, Lance Howard, Bob Kellow, 'Spam' Spafford, Mick Martin, 'Tammy' Simpson, Jack Leggo, Dave Shannon, Bob Hay

several yards from the bar and was just about to make a flying leap in an attempt to clear the counter in one wild lunge when Guy Gibson intervened.

'Perhaps later Toby,' he said quietly. 'It's time to eat now.' Those simple words saved the day, and probably a broken neck for Toby. At the mention of food a smile crossed his rugged features. Within five minutes he was consuming an excellent lunch.

I have ever been amazed at the small number of casualties following some of these 'parties' held by RAF operational squadrons. Toby Foxlee once drove through closed level crossing gates in his MG two-seater. The gates were damaged, but not Toby! I have seen black eyes and cut lips; I have even seen a fellow climb down a drainpipe, from three stories up, like a cat burglar and this after drinking steadily for four hours, but never with serious consequences, strangely enough. Always so near and yet so far.

On this particular occasion, after lunch, Guy Gibson made a short speech, much to the delight of the mixed company. His final reference was to the party to be given by A. V. Roe's that evening. He insinuated that we should all go to bed and prepare for our final fling. I thought it was good advice, for I was still feeling the effects of the previous night. I found Les Munro and asked him if he was coming along. He also thought it a sound scheme and at approximately four o'clock that afternoon, we clambered into bed. If it seems to be all drink and sleep, it is no more than a true description of a bomber squadron celebration. From the point of view of the air-crew lads, it merely meant grasping a few hours respite before, to use their own phrase, 'dicing with death' again. I, as an accepted and proud member of 617 Squadron, was merely dragged along in a whirlpool, against which I had no resistance. Frankly, I never attempted to resist. As long as I was able to do justice to my position when at the office desk, I felt no cause to reproach myself. I think I can proudly say that I never let the side down, either at the bar or behind the desk! In a squadron one was amazed at the amount of liquor consumed. Now the war is over I can admit that my capacity was possibly over-estimated, for I poured many a drink down the lavatory, or into a plant pot. Hence my apparent unlimited capacity.

Les and I woke just after 6.30 pm, neither of us feeling like any further parties. However, after a cold shower we felt much better. The venue for the party was the *Hungaria* in Regent Street. When we arrived most of the guests were already there. I spotted T. O. M. Sopwith; Mr (now Sir) Roy Chadwick; the Lancaster designer Sir Roy Dobson; A. V. Roe's managing director and the newly promoted Air Commodore J. N. H. Whitworth, not to mention the guest of honour Wing Commander Guy Gibson, and a very studious looking gentleman, Mr Barnes Wallis, the designer of the missile responsible for the shattering of the dams. He looked rather out of place amid all the drinking and loud conversation. Many other famous personages were in the company, all intent on paying homage to the stocky 'Wingco' and his men.

The company was not entirely composed of famous characters. There were the other type of 'back room boys' – the ground crew; NCOs representing their own men on this auspicious occasion. FltSgt Gover, FltSgt Smith, Sgt Cummack, Sgt Heveron, FltSgt Powell and others. FltLt Caple and FO Watson, the Engineering and Armament officer respectively were there, all having fun prior to returning to the more serious business of servicing the mighty Lancasters. It was an excellent dinner, the wine and food was of the very best.

A spirit of good fellowship pervaded the atmosphere. Menus began to circulate amongst the guests, for all present to sign, in memory of this great occasion. The cover referred to the 'Damn-Busters', not 'Dam busters'. Whether this was accident of design I don't know. I still have my copy and it is one of my proudest possessions.

After cigars had been handed round the company was called to order by Mr T. O. M. Sopwith. He made an excellent speech before presenting Wing Commander Gibson with a beautifully modelled silver Lancaster Aircraft. I can almost see the presentation now, just as if it had occurred only yesterday instead of many years ago. The Wing Commander's face was a study, a mixture of pride and embarrassment. He stammered a little but recovered when the boys shouted, 'Speech, speech.'

He only made a short speech, but in a very few words paid tribute to all those who had made the great 'dam raid' possible. As usual he was thorough, including every participant, from 'the back room boys' to the lowliest 'erk' and to the workers in the

Guy Gibson being presented with a model Lancaster by T.O.M. Sopwith. Seated right is Group Captain Whitworth.

great A. V. Roe plant. He finally sat down amid thunderous applause, his youthful face flushed.

Other speeches followed, all paying tribute to the 'little man' and his comrades. I felt as if I were taking part in a little event in the history books of our country. I don't suppose this is true really, for historians rarely include occasions such as this in their records! Perhaps they should! It could make future generations realise that our fighting men are flesh and blood, just normal men with normal weaknesses. There are many books about the exploits of our war heroes. I don't like terms such as 'young men with old eyes', or 'prematurely aged'. The aircrew boys were quite normal – tired, depressed, happy, and sometimes scared, just like any other person, in any other fighting force.

After the final speech we all settled down to celebrate in earnest but before this a further presentation was made, this time to the inventor of the mine, Sir Barnes Wallis. He was given a large photograph of the Möhne Dam, autographed by the entire party. I saw him blow his nose unnecessarily hard. He was no doubt, very proud, and envied. We would all have given a lot to be in possession of such a memento. From then on the fun waxed fast and furious. We had an extra special surprise, when 'Mick' Martin, our 'ace' Australian pilot, came in with a party of theatrical celebrities. In the company were Arthur Askey, Pat Taylor, Jack Train, Eddie Gray and Chesney Allen.

They were grand and provided us with at least an hour's first class entertainment. In between turns by the 'funny men', Jack Hylton played the piano and Pat Taylor sang sentimental songs. I found myself arm in arm with a fellow I had never seen before, and didn't care. Neither did he for that matter and I found out afterwards that he was a famous newspaper cartoonist. The evening wore on and the bottles were slowly emptied. We sang RAF songs, 1914–18 war songs, dirty songs and nursery rhymes. Eyes glazed, and knees sagged. Nature began to come into its own again, and though the spirit of the company was quite willing, the contents of the many empty bottles had played havoc with the flesh!

The Wing Commander wished me a very hazy goodnight, as did several others. Handshaking was going on all around and I have some very vague recollections of my arm being pumped up and down on numerous occasions. I only know that the worthy Munro grabbed me, and escorted me back to the hotel. In spite of his vehement insistence that he was perfectly sober, both he and I went to bed in our trousers!

The end of a great day!

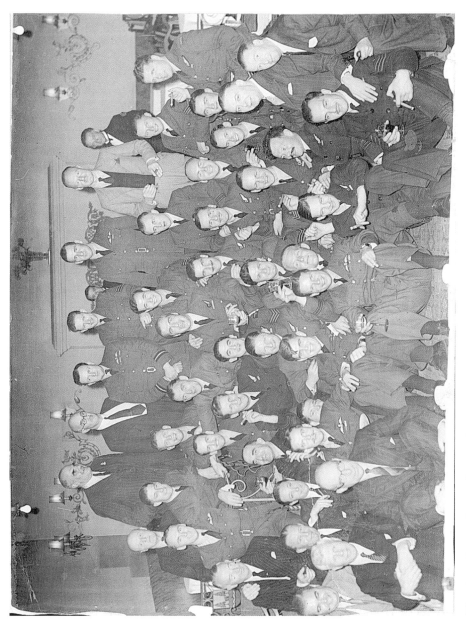

The Avro Party. Guy Gibson is bottom centre; Barnes Wallis is bottom left

5 BACK TO BUSINESS

I won't go into the hangover business again, but it was obviously present the next morning. However this was our day to return to the common task, so I was looking forward to a normal and undisturbed good night's sleep.

We had a special train to take us back to Lincoln. The scene at King's Cross for this return journey was in marked contrast to the outward run. The chaps had capitulated entirely. Each carriage was full of recumbent dozing figures. You could have heard the proverbial pin drop. I may mention that it was only a matter of minutes before I too joined the company of silent men. There would be no painting the town of Lincoln red that night!

Everything went according to plan. Transport met us at Lincoln, and there were no casualties to report. We were duly deposited at Scampton and most of the fellows went straight to bed. The Lancasters were still waiting for their next trip, just as we had left them. It was back to grim reality and war again.

The AOC had granted the Squadron two days' rest for the Investiture. Who knows; tomorrow he may give the order for a maximum effort attack. He couldn't afford to be sentimental.

As it happened there was no war for 617 Squadron tomorrow, or at all in the month of June. The boys didn't like it very much. Other squadrons were working night after night. Wing Commander Gibson was taking a well-earned leave and it was becoming increasingly difficult for his deputy, Dave Maltby, to prevent discontent creeping into the ranks.

The ground crew were also beginning to be affected. They were fed up with the inactivity, and were finding it hard to face the jibes of their counterparts of the other squadrons. The 'one op' gag was no longer funny and unless something was done it looked as though open warfare would soon be declared in the local bars. Eventually Wing Commander Gibson returned from leave. He sensed the trouble and immediately organised sport and competitive flying practice with a promise of plenty of work to come. He took part in all the flying himself, in preparation for future operations, but he was living in a fool's paradise. He had been recalled to form 617 Squadron and lead the 'Dam Raid' but the C-in-C had no intention of allowing him to continue operational flying.

It all happened at once, as it usually does in the service. One minute you feel snug and secure, the next you find yourself on your way to the other end of the earth. Information came through that 'Gibby' was destined to visit America, in the company of none other than the Prime Minister, the Right Honourable Mr Winston Churchill. Another Squadron Leader was posted in, presumably to take over the reins from the Wing Commander. This was Squadron Leader George Holden DSO, DFC – a low-flying 'ace' from Number 4 Bomber Group.

The Wing Commander did not leave right away, as originally expected, but spent two weeks hard at it, briefing George Holden on the intricacies of commanding a special duties squadron. George had no crew and the Wing Commander offered him his boys, who would now be spare. This was readily accepted by George, but the crew were not so overjoyed when they heard the news. Quite frankly, they did not like the idea of another pilot, after having flown with the 'Wingco', but like the grand crowd they were, they accepted the Commanding Officer's decision without further ado. That decision cost most of them their lives only a few short weeks after, just as the decision to fly again on operations cost Guy Gibson his life in the winter of 1944.

Such decisions cannot be criticised, for in war they just have to be made. It is the final result that counts after all is over. Guy Gibson's last active task with the Squadron was on 15th July. At last we were to operate.

The battle order was printed showing Wing Commander Gibson as Officer in charge of night flying. Italy was the place our crews were to visit. They were to attack two different targets in that country and then fly on to Blida in North Africa to refuel. The length of the flight was such that the petrol tanks would be two-thirds empty when the target was reached. It was therefore impossible to return direct to base. The crews were delighted at the prospect of a visit to the 'dark continent'. The only person far from thrilled was Guy Gibson himself. He did give all the boys a cheery goodbye prior to take-off, but as we drove to the marshalling point he gave vent to his feelings.

'If there is anything I hate Adj. it's watching other people go to war. I like the idea of going to America, but I'd sooner bloody well fly with my own Squadron.' He grimaced, 'Ah well, what the hell….'

We watched the Lancasters trundle into the darkening sky. After the last one thundered away Gibson stood for some time listening to the roar of it's engines. Gradually the roar diminished into a distant drone….then silence. With a sigh the Wing Commander turned to me.

'Well that's it Adj. Come on, let's go and have a beer.' He added distantly, half to himself, 'I've always wanted to see Algiers too.'

The rest of the evening was without incident. The Wing Commander did not have to stay out of bed very long, as is often the lot of OC Night Flying. This was because we knew that there would be no early returning machines, and as the flight was non-stop to Africa, it was out of our hands.

From then on, our great little Squadron Commander drifted out of the picture as far as 617 Squadron was concerned. He was very rarely available at Scampton, being fully occupied in his preparations for the visit to the States. In actual fact, he just disappeared from the scene, and then the next thing we knew he was in America. He left 617 Squadron without fanfares of trumpets or ceremonial parades, but both he and his men preferred it that way. It wasn't as if he was forgotten, far from it. Many a time on routine inspections, I came across newspaper cuttings and photographs, pinned or pasted to the walls of barrack huts. The photographs were of Gibson, and the press cuttings outlined his movements in America. Guy Gibson was not forgotten and never will be, as long as there is one man or woman left who knew him.

The return from operation against the crumbling Italian bastion was more like a return from a shopping trip. I suppose regulations say that aircrew should not bring any goods or chattels back from a foreign clime, without a Customs declaration. If I thought the boys had done any grievous wrong I should not record it here but it wasn't as if they had come back with priceless articles. They couldn't very well, for they had been allowed to take only a limited amount of cash.

I met the machines at their dispersal points, in the hours of 25th July 1943. I found it hard to believe my eyes. Piled against each Lancaster there were many items we had not seen for a long time – oranges, onions, dates were abundant. Heated discussions were in progress as to ownership. Aircrew kept passing me in dirty khaki drill, arms full of boodle, one chap having a garland of onions around his neck. I spotted Micky Martin wearing a red fez. I approached him.

'Well Mick, how did it go?' I asked.

'Piece of cake Adj., piece of cake.' His face was burned red with African sun. He added, 'I could do with a bloody bath though, I don't think they ever wash in Africa.'

He turned and lashed out at Toby Foxlee, his rear gunner. 'They happen to be oranges runt!' and so it went on, until the evidence of Africa was just a few rotten oranges, lying squashed under the wings of the Lancasters.

There was another trip to Africa that month. It was a 'special leaflet raid', much to the disgust of everyone. Joe McCarthy voiced his sentiments.

'Like selling god-damned newspapers,' he said.

In spite of all the grumbling there was plenty of competition amongst the crews to appear on the battle order. Those who had already visited Africa wanted to go again, and those who had not yet been, were curious to see the country. Once again we operated without loss, and the aircraft returned, again loaded with fruit, but this time some of it smelt a trifle high. Apparently the machines had been standing by for favourable weather in Africa, stacked with perishable goods, and the hot sun beating on the metal fuselages did little to preserve the fruit. Apparently the sand, heat, and bugs were no longer appreciated by the crews, for the remarks heard in the mess, when the conversation drifted to Africa, were hardly complimentary. However, these brief visits provided excellent opportunities for the 'line shooters' to air their superiority in the local taverns. I heard many stories which started as quite normal anecdotes finish up with so many trimmings and additions, that they were hardly recognisable as the original.

6   REMEMBER THE DEAD

It was now August 1943. It seemed a long while since the original spectacular attack on the dams. Guy Gibson had left us and George Holden was now in charge. Life in the squadron drifted along in a pleasant almost domesticated manner. Some of the fellows liked it like this, and a few, mostly the inexperienced, thought it was a waste of time. The famous Squadron! Overestimated, they thought. It wasn't to be long before they were proved wrong. This pleasant, quiet period was for 617 Squadron, merely a short reprieve. Perhaps it was as well that the crews were in ignorance of their next task. It would not be pleasant to know that one had only a few weeks to live. The single difference between the life of an average bomber crew and a condemned man was that the bomber boys didn't know the date. I put it like that, because I don't want people to forget just what they owe to these men.

For us now, the war has been over for years, and we can carry out our daily tasks, thanks to them. For some of us it is difficult. Perhaps the future does not seem too bright, but after all we have a future of a kind. Take a cross section of the Squadron during this August of 1943 and see how some of the boys were planning for their future, a future that was never to be.

Take Bob Hutcheson, my own friend. He was always over at Boston to see his girl friend. This stocky dark haired Liverpool boy was really in love, and often used to tell me of his plans. He decided not to get married until he had finally ceased operations, a decision apparently shared by his girl. I often spent an evening with them, and could not help but feel, on those occasions, that they were both scared something would separate them. Bob wasn't the type who indulged in riotous living like many of the boys. He was a total abstainer, and spent most of his time writing, playing tennis or football, indulging occasionally in amateur theatricals. Whatever he did was of no matter for in September 1943 he died in a blazing aircraft. He left behind his girl, and heartbroken parents, and a glittering Distinguished Flying Cross, plus a shiny bar. So instead of a son, Mr and Mrs Hutcheson have a medal, and a memory.

Dave Maltby, the genial flight commander of A Flight, was also very much in love – with his wife. He lived at Woodhall Spa, not far from Scampton. They had a son, Johnny, of whom they were justly proud. A happy-go-lucky fellow was Dave, and a fearless pilot. Dave and Nina were a wonderful partnership. They were both aware of the danger to their wonderful rosy love affair, but ignored it completely. Again, to no avail. David crashed into the sea in September 1943. His body was picked up by the RAF Air Sea Rescue service just off Cromer. Another world tumbled into ruins. I met Mrs Maltby months after – she still couldn't believe that it had happened.

In Maltby's crew there was a boy named Stone – a Sergeant Wireless Operator. He went down with the plane. A day after the incident a frail middle-aged lady was shown into my office. She was Sergeant Stone's mother. Through trembling lips she explained that he was her only boy. Bravely stifling the tears she kept repeating one question. 'Did he suffer?' The poor lady was so dazed that she hardly realised where she was, and still less how she was going to get back home. In fact there was no train that afternoon, so I had to fix up accommodation in the local village. I felt awful throughout the interview, particularly when she said, 'It is something to know that we have such brave men as you left to carry on the fight.' The only battle I ever fought was against an overpowering amount of official letters and forms. I tried to explain but she didn't understand. Poor Mrs Stone, she didn't even have a medal to cherish. Perhaps that doesn't really matter?

Les Knight was a dam raid DSO pilot. This Australian, a pleasant faced boy, used to write reams of letters home to his native land. His idea of a hectic night out was a visit to the cinema. He had no affairs as far as I know, merely a burning desire to return home when his job was done. He talked a lot about sheep farming so maybe that was included in his post war planning. He used to fill in a lot of application forms for jobs in Australia, presumably to take one of them up on his release from the RAAF. No matter. He never saw Australia again, but perished in his aircraft alone, after saving his crew. Thus a gap was torn into another homestead, swiftly, and without warning.

Our Present CO, George Holden, was also to lose his life. During the month of August, he was happily engaged in the task of filling Guy Gibson's shoes, fully alive to his responsibilities and making a good job of it. He was planning a future in the RAF, often referring to himself jokingly as the future 'Group Captain' Holden. He is buried somewhere near Nordhorn in Germany.

Others I can think of are FltLt 'Jimmy' Wilson; 'Bill' Divall, and FltLt Ralph Allsebrook. They pressed home attacks with glorious tenacity over German territory, and paid the full price. Of their plans I know nothing. Perhaps they didn't have any. Perhaps it is just as well they didn't.

Then there are those who survived. Joe McCarthy the giant American; Munro, the laconic New Zealander; Shannon and Martin both from Australia. Whenever I think of 617 Squadron I think of these boys. They volunteered to come to us, and with us they flew their hearts out. They were obviously making plans for our Brave New World, but would they be able to fulfil them? Would Joe return to his post as US lifesaver on Long Island US? Would the lads from down under return to farming or offices? They might have if those who watched the war being fought remembered those who actually fought it, and accepted them as men, capable men, instead of an embarrassment.

These are just a few names from the scrapbook of 617 Squadron. There were many others, equally worthy of mention, who were with us in August 1943. Some perished bravely like their comrades whose names I have already mentioned, and others lived on to see the peace.

7   CONINGSBY

We moved from Scampton that month. It was a bit of a blow to us all, for we were happy there. We liked the place, and we liked Air Commodore Whitworth, who had been promoted to Base Commander. However, orders said we had to go, so that was that. Our new abode was to be Coningsby, another 'drome in Lincolnshire. This, incidentally, was my first experience of organising the move of a full Royal Air Force Unit, and what a job! Meetings, conferences, paperwork, parades, and even a flight in a Tiger Moth were needed to complete arrangements at Coningsby. George Holden took me in this machine, and nearly frightened me to death. On the way over I was sitting in the front cockpit, quite enjoying myself, strapped in, and smothered in huge goggles. I felt quite a hero. Suddenly there was a splutter, and the small propeller spun slowly to a standstill. Down went the nose of the 'Tiger', and simultaneously down went my heart into my shoes. I had no parachute, and I couldn't see George Holden from my position in the front. The ground came closer and closer as we fell like a stricken butterfly. I kept telling myself that we wouldn't hit the ground very hard in such a light machine. Suddenly I looked up, and on my port side there was a little mirror, like a driving mirror on a car. I could see George in the rear cockpit grinning all over his face, revelling in my misery. Then I realised all was well, and that he had stalled the motor on purpose – all for my benefit. He started up again, needless to say, before we reached the ground. He did this once more before we touched down at Coningsby, but this time I did not worry.

We did our business at Coningsby quite rapidly, but when George came and asked me if I was ready for take off, I decided I had more work to do and went back later by road! Perhaps it was as well, for Holden told me later that he had spent a considerable amount of time practising 'looping the loop' over Scampton, before he finally landed. He was crazy enough to drop me out of the cockpit, and apologise later!

By the end of the month the move was complete. Thus we severed our connections with Scampton, our first home. We were made very welcome at Coningsby for we were the first Squadron they had seen there for some time, due to the fact that the airfield had been closed in order to facilitate the construction of concrete runways. It wasn't long before the boys settled in, and soon Boston instead of Lincoln became the rendezvous of 617 Squadron. Many romances started in Lincoln died a natural death, as fresh ones started under the shadow of the dignified Boston Stump.

So from June to August we had had a big party, lost our popular Wing Commander, completed a few minor operations, without loss, had our fun and moved to a new home. Quiet and peaceful I suppose, but who would begrudge these fellows brief periods of respite. I didn't, for I had been in Bomber Command long enough to know that the saying 'here today – gone tomorrow' could be anything but humorous.

We had not been at Coningsby very long before it became apparent that 617 Squadron had once again been earmarked for a 'special job'. Day after day George Holden was to be seen in conference with men, both service and civilian, who were complete strangers to us all. Heavy lorries were to be seen arriving at the bomb dump, laden with ominous looking shapes, covered with tarpaulins. It's funny how everyone is aware that something is going to happen on an operational station, even if they have no concrete evidence.

When I say 'concrete evidence', that is not strictly true. The armourers and mechanics began to work very late, sometimes long into the night, as did the instrument repairers and electricians. A flight of Mosquito aircraft from a night fighter squadron arrived at the airfield. All these things add up, and the average Squadron man, though he knows nothing definite, senses enough to stir his blood with the thought of the approaching 'something'.

All flying training was now carried out under the cover of darkness, and practically every evening a formation of low flying Lancasters, accompanied by Mosquitos, roared across the flat Lincolnshire countryside. I used to watch them from my little office, feeling something like one of the actors in the film *Target for Tonight*. Strangely enough, when I first saw that film, the story of a Wellington bomber and its crew, I was not a member of the Royal Air Force, but I looked forward to that day when I hoped I would become a great-coated officer. I also fondly imagined myself issuing instructions to thousands of men, the originator of battle orders. I did in a way achieve part of this ambition. I signed battle orders, but never originated them!

In spite of the very small part played by an individual when he is a member of His Majesty's Forces in war-time, it is, never-the-less an essential part, whatever the task may be. In my own particular capacity as a pen-pushing administrator, being an integral part of a Bomber Squadron never failed to thrill me. I was proud to be a tiny cog in this gigantic wheel. It inserted into my vertebrae a lot of solid substance, which I fear was lacking prior to my appearance in uniform. I am glad to be a civilian again, but in spite of any opposition I will always advocate that a young man should don the King's uniform for a certain period of his life, even if it is only brief.

On September 14th 1943 Squadron Leader Holden instructed me to produce a Battle Order for that night. It read as follows:

> SqnLdr Holden & Crew.
> SqnLdr Maltby & Crew
> FltLt Knight & Crew
> FltLt Shannon & Crew
> FltLt Wilson & Crew
> FltLt Allsebrook & Crew
> FO Rice & Crew
> FO Divall & Crew

plus six Mosquito night fighter crew as escort detailed by their Commanding Officer.

This was to be a picture-book attack on the Dortmund Ems Canal. Our aircraft were to carry 12,000lb 'cookies' for the first time. The idea was that a certain strip of the canal was to be breached by the apparently simple method of placing these huge bombs at regular intervals in the soft soil at the side of the water. They would be delayed action, and on detonation the eight holes made by the bombs would join together, forming one gaping rent in the side of this vital German waterway. The success of the attack of course depended on its accuracy, and our boys were confident they could do it.

The aircraft took off to schedule. Tragedy however was to overtake us this night.

Within an hour we received news that our machines were returning to base because of unfavourable weather conditions and, worst of all, one of them had crashed into the sea off Cromer. All was confusion for some time. The Lancasters began to land at Coningsby and garbled reports on the ill-fated aircraft began to circulate.

Eventually the truth became apparent. Our own Dave Maltby had gone. By some wicked stroke of misfortune he had hit the sea and in spite of very good work on the part of Brian Goodale, Shannon's wireless operator, only one body, that of Dave Maltby himself, had been found by the Air Sea Rescue launch.

The thought that Dave, Jock Fort his bombardier, all of this cheery crew, had gone affected us deeply. It was difficult to imagine that never again would we see the bulky figure of Maltby lifting a pewter tankard to his mouth. Normally the crews would have celebrated an 'abortive' by having a happy drinking party in the Mess. On this evening, groups of men stood about talking in hushed whispers. George Holden, now acting CO had the worst task of all. He had to visit Mrs Maltby in the neighbouring village of Woodhall and tell her that the happy-go-lucky husband of hers would no longer be catching her in his powerful arms, and little Johnny, their son, would never again be tossed ceilingwards by his proud father. Poor George. It was also the last night of his life.

Now I look back on that September I really think it was the most miserable month of my life. It was just as if a bomb had dropped in our midst, leaving me a dazed and bewildered survivor, surrounded by the mangled bodies of my family. I think that describes it well.

15th September 1943 – that was the blackest day in the history of 617 Squadron. Yet from the weather point of view it was very bright and, like healthy young animals, the aircrew boys had shaken off the depression of the night before, with the exception, perhaps, of George Holden, who I thought looked tired and ill. He always managed a gallant smile, in spite of his innermost feelings, every time I saw him that day.

The raid was to be a further attempt at the canal. The only alteration to the Battle Order was the inclusion of FltLt Martin, in place of Dave Maltby. Take off time approached, and as usual I wandered around the crew rooms, watching the men clambering into flying kit, a sight which always thrilled me. I remember seeing Bill Divall playing cowboys and indians with his crew. He was wearing an Irvine jacket and he had a knife down one boot and his revolver down the other. Bob Hutcheson, my friend, and the Signals Leader, an ex-member of Guy Gibson's Dam Buster crew, waved to me.

'I'll be coming up to your office in a minute, Adj.,' he said. 'I want you to keep my keys until tomorrow.'

After a further browse around I went back to my office and Bob Hutcheson followed shortly afterwards. As he entered, he gave me his usual peculiar little salute. It was rather funny really, for Bob always paid me the courtesy of a salute even though we were close friends. We talked about this and that while he sat on the edge of my desk. At last he moved towards the door.

'Well, must be going, see you tomorrow, Humph.' Again that funny little salute, and so went Bob. I never saw him again.

Soon the hubbub in the building died down, to be replaced by the reverberating roar of the Merlin engines. After take off I watched the eight Lancasters take up position and fly across the airfield in tight formation. They were rather difficult to see, for the night was dark, but with lights on their wings and tails it was just possible to discern the silhouettes against the night sky.

I watched the lights out of sight and then decided to go back to my office, and work for a while. When I entered the door I saw I had two visitors, big Joe McCarthy and Les Munro. They both looked as miserable as sin.

'What the devil is the matter with you two?' I asked.

Munro merely grunted. Joe was more excitable. 'Just to think I have to sit around and twiddle my god-damn thumbs, while the boys are out. It sure burns me up.'

Les and Joe were both 'ace' pilots, but had been temporarily grounded on the instructions of the medical officer. Joe was in charge of night flying.

'Well, it can't be helped chaps,' I said lamely.

Joe heaved his huge bulk out of my chair. 'I'm going to sit over in the watch office,' he said. 'Are either of you two coming?'

I hadn't intended to leave the office for some time, but I felt like company and I knew I should get first hand information if I joined forces with these two. So off we all went. The watch office always impressed me, and always reminded me of an operating theatre, particularly at night. The room was shrouded in sinister half-light but one could discern the hunched figures of the WAAFs and airmen on watch. The Officer-in-Command nodded in our direction as we entered, his face looking like a pale smudge. The powerful wireless sets crackled and popped, waiting to pick up any sound from aircraft wishing to land at Coningsby.

We all sat down and prepared to wait. I didn't stay put for long, I couldn't. I spent long periods on the balcony outside the tower, gazing into the night sky, straining my ears for the drone of returning machines. An hour or two must have passed when McCarthy came rushing out on to the balcony.

'We've lost George Holden, Adj.,' he panted. 'Shot down just over the German frontier, a place called Nordhorn.'

I just said, 'Good God,' and added 'that takes care of most of Gibby's crew, Mac.' 'Yeah, I know,' said the big American, 'poor old Spam.' He said 'poor old Spam', because in all instances like this one thought of one's personal friends first.

I thought 'poor old Hutch.' No more salutes, no more tennis, no more stage shows. The night suddenly became cold and chilly.

I said, 'Any more news, Mac?'

'Very little,' he said, 'but I reckon we are going to take a beating tonight.' He added, 'Les Knight signalled back that he was in trouble – lost two engines. He is going to try and return to base on the other two. I haven't much hope somehow. It's a damn long way on four, never mind about two.'

We both lapsed into silence. Eventually Mac left me and went in search of further information in his capacity as Officer-in-Charge of Night Flying. Both he and Munro joined me some little time later. It was difficult to see the expression on their faces but I sensed that all was not well.

I said, 'Well,' in what I imagined to be an offhand manner.

This time Les Munro spoke, his New Zealand twang sounding funny to me. He droned, 'Reckon we shan't see many of the boys back tonight. Something went wrong with our picture book operation. Apart from George Holden we have possibly lost three or four others.' He raised his voice, 'This is bloody awful, sitting here and doing nothing – just waiting, and waiting.'

Presently we heard the drone of aircraft. Soon there were two or three circling the airfield, but they were not the Lancasters. They were the Mosquitos, the night fighter escort, obviously back first by virtue of their superior speed.

We were soon in possession of further facts from these pilots. The CO, a Squadron Leader, gave us details in a few terse sentences.

'It was terrible,' he said. 'We couldn't see a damned thing owing to thick ground mist, and all the time the Jerry flak positions were knocking hell out of the Lancs.' He shivered, 'It was like groping in the dark – blind man's buff, only much more dangerous. We were all milling around there, trying to hit something we couldn't see, and every so often there would be a terrific barrage which ceased as quickly as it started. It didn't stop quickly enough however, for I saw at least two bombers blow up and later saw the wreckage burning on the ground.' He shook his head sadly, 'I guess we weren't much good to you chaps tonight.' He then walked off mumbling … 'couldn't see a damn thing.'

We still waited and hoped, and soon one Lancaster came into the circuit. It was David Shannon, true to his reputation, back first. A short time after, Micky Martin landed, followed by Jeff Rice. After that, silence and we were to see or hear no more of the remaining five machines.

I went back to the Mess, tired and upset. I didn't want to say or do anything. Five out of eight machines. Five out of eight, and the operation was a failure! We didn't scratch the Dortmund Ems. It was to be several years before the job our boys tried to do was actually completed. It wouldn't have been so bad if the lads could have succeeded in their task, but to think that these young flying boys had been cut to ribbons … for what? I began to mentally count off the pilots. Allsebrook, Divall, Knight, Wilson and George Holden. I was musing to myself and without knowing it passed the Station Commander's room in the Officers Mess. On hearing the Group Captains voice address me, I came out of my dream.

He was very kind. He called me in and offered me a whisky. I accepted gratefully, for now the reaction of this horrible night was really beginning to get a grip of me, and I was having great difficulty controlling my limbs.

Group Captain Patch OBE, affectionately known as 'Sam', must have had a good idea of how I was feeling, for he chatted to me quietly for some time, talking about anything but flying. The only time he actually mentioned it was when he rose, signifying that the interview was at an end. He placed his arm on my shoulder.

'Never mind old lad,' he said, 'you'll forget in time. You've got to.'

I am not going to say that I felt much better with these words. I didn't. I crawled into my bed, and spent the remaining hours of the night trying to sleep, without much success.

The next day came the casualty procedure – those horrible telegrams again. The temporary Commanding Officer of 617 Squadron was Flight Lieutenant H. B. 'Micky' Martin, one of the survivors of the previous evening. This made it doubly difficult, for Micky knew little or nothing about RAF administration. However, we plodded on, ably assisted by the old guard, Sergeant Heveron, and Flight Sergeant Powell. Later that day, news came through that Micky Martin was a Squadron Leader with effect immediately. On top of that, we were to operate again that night. With a scramble we could raise a maximum effort of twelve crews, the three from the previous night, plus nine practically new ones. I was led to understand that this attack had been 'laid on' as a bolster to the Squadron morale, which could rapidly crumble after the previous night's devastating losses.

The target was the Antheor Viaduct in the South of France. This entailed another trip to Africa. As it happened all went well this time, and the aircraft crews returned to base within a few days, without loss. It was difficult to imagine that we were a Squadron at all. I could remember Guy Gibson's words, when he said we should either make history or be wiped out. Another raid like Dortmund Ems, and we should be practically non-existent. Apparently our fate was being discussed at a high level. Some of the big men thought it unwise to proceed with the policy of a Special Squadron, whilst others, using the 'Dam Raid' as a lever, thought we should be reinforced. The latter gained the day, and accordingly the Squadrons in 5 Group were instructed by the Air Officer Commanding to each send two of their best crews to 617.

Some of the crews that arrived were pleased to come, but one or two were not quite so happy. Micky Martin interviewed them all, and any crew voicing objections to joining 617 was returned to their unit immediately. It was a slow and painful process, and even this arrangement did not give us all the crews required. After a week we had added only four crews to our strength, FltLt O'Shaugnessy, FO Weedon, PO Willsher and WO Bull.

I, from my point of view, couldn't help but feel that we were only half a unit. A full Bomber Squadron should be at least twenty crews, with four in reserve, and here we were with less than a round dozen, most of them inexperienced. I wouldn't go as far as to say that our morale had gone. It couldn't with a live wire like Micky Martin at the helm, but we were a trifle bedraggled.

The month of October 1943 was a nightmare. We didn't operate, but merely seemed to live an aimless sort of existence while all around us the remainder of the Group attacked Germany night after night. Most of the boys went to Boston to drown their sorrows at night. I began to wonder if we were doomed to be disbanded.

8   A NEW CO

In November of that year we turned the corner when news was received that we were to have a Wing Commander posted in to take over, a man who had been a Group Captain, and had thrown his rank away to fly again. It was none other than Leonard Cheshire, a famous name in the Royal Air Force. I wondered what he would be like. I imagined a snooty individual who would possibly arrive cracking the whip. Mick Martin also wondered, and seemed to be sad at the prospect of losing his command. He knew it was only temporary but he had enjoyed every moment of it.

Cheshire arrived. He walked into my office. I sprang up from my chair and waited. His voice was soft and pleasant, he held out his hand.

'I'm Cheshire,' he said. 'Glad to meet you, I've heard quite a bit about you.'

I think I must have swelled visibly.

'Pleased to meet you, sir,' I stuttered.

'Now then Adj., I think we have a lot to do. I'll leave the paper work to you but apparently we need crews – urgently.' He turned and addressed Martin who stood behind him.

'I think we'll have a conference now Mick, if you don't mind.'

Martin answered, 'Certainly sir.'

I thought it was rather remarkable that the new Wing Commander should address Martin as 'Mick' so soon, but I was soon to find out that he was always like that. You couldn't help but like this pleasant, slim ex-Varsity man. He always will remain in my mind as the perfect RAF officer. He knew how to get the very best out of everyone with the least possible effort. His manner of obtaining this maximum efficiency with minimum effort was by setting a perfect example himself, both in the air and on the ground. A born leader, I suppose.

When he arrived at Coningsby he had no crew, but, as if by magic, he built one around his own person. A typical Cheshire crew too, devoted to their Captain, and he was very proud of them. In Wing Commander Cheshire's makeup there was a streak of humour a yard wide. He would get up to all sorts of tricks, from asking me to hold the driving wheel of his car when I was sitting in the passenger seat, while he would carry on an animated conversation with others sitting in the back of the vehicle, to frightening the life out of his crew by leaving the aircraft solely on the automatic pilot while he had a walk around on some pretext or other. He told me once that his sole ambition was to have a car with the driving wheel in reverse, so he could drive a car around London backwards to see the effect on the natives! A loveable crazy character!

From the arrival of Cheshire we began to recuperate, a bit like a wounded animal licking its wounds. Replacements began to arrive slowly, the first one being a Canadian, SqnLdr Suggitt, DFC. He assumed command of 'A' Flight. One notable character posted to 617 Squadron during this period was Flying Officer 'Gerry' Witherick, DFM. I didn't know too much about him then, but I should imagine that at the cessation of hostilities he had one of the most impressive records ever held by an air gunner in the Royal Air Force. He flew with anyone, any time, anywhere, and was literally un-killable, if there is such a phrase. I remember attending a party to celebrate his one-hundredth trip as an air gunner. He always said that being an air gunner was the easiest way he had ever found to earn a living! When I look back on those days with 617 Squadron, I think his name stands out equally as brightly as the famous men who led us. He was the Churchill of air gunners!

Gerry was shot down after the *Tirpitz* raid. His pilot, Willy Carey, managed to land in Sweden and he sent me a letter from the *Astoria Hotel* in Stockholm.

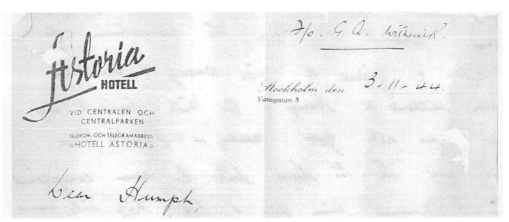

I hope you are fit and well and drinking plenty.
All the boys are all right except Willy who hurt his knee when we landed – I must
say the conduct of the entire crew was excellent – there was no panic and everyone did

their job quietly and efficiently – especially Willy who made the sweetest forced landing you've ever been in.

We were badly hit in the bomb doors and port and starboard wings and three petrol tanks were holed, and the port inner had to be feathered while petrol was streaming past my turret like nobody's business, but in spite of that young Willy just shoved her over the mountains into Sweden and picked a nice swamp to put her down without a bump – the kite burned up but we all got away – Willy's knee was cut to the bone but he never complained. I bound him up and took him into some high ground and covered him with parachutes and lit a fire. After many adventures we finally reached Stockholm where we are patiently waiting to come and see you.

Please give my regards to Mr Tait, Freddy Watts – Paddy Gingles and the boys and tell them I'll be seeing you soon. Also tell Tony to look after Basil properly – I hope our kit hasn't been mislaid too much.

Cheerio Humph,
All the best from,
Gerry

Witherick was awarded a DFC after completing 100 sorties. He already held the DFM. Willy Carey survived the war but was killed in a car accident in Australia.

FltLt R.E.G. Youseman, D.F.C, captained another of our newer crews. He came to us with a grand record, and was mad keen on flying. So mad in fact that he was always talking about it, and many a time did he have to duck when someone pitched a cushion in his direction as a form of objection to 'shop' in the mess. He lost his life on 17th November 1943 after operating against the Antheor Viaduct once again. It is not known how it happened. Apparently he landed in North Africa after completing his attack. He took off to return to base with the other crews, but from then on nothing further was heard. It is believed that he crashed into the Mediterranean sea, possibly due to engine trouble. Poor Ted, he would have sooner died in the thick of battle Tragically, he had two passengers, RAF personnel returning to the UK for leave, in fact 'hitch hiking' an air lift home.

December arrived without any further loss and it appeared that our 'family life' was to resume. The powers above did not seem to be cooking up anything special for the boys. Since the Dortmund Ems I was constantly hoping that all our future attacks would be simpler in character, for I feared a repetition of those devastating losses.

One morning early in the month the Wing Commander rang for me. I could tell from his manner that it was another 'mystery trip'.

'Special call from Tempsford, Adj. Four crews. They will be McCarthy, Clayton, Weedon and Bull. Detachment will last for approximately a week. Will you make all the arrangements?'

I said, 'Yes sir,' and as if in answer to my unspoken question he said, 'I don't know much more than that myself, I'll tell Joe McCarthy. He'll be OC for the detachment. There will be a number of ground crew going too. Caple will give you their names. OK?'

'Very good sir,' I said and went off to make the arrangements.

RAF Station Tempsford was one of the RAF stations constantly shrouded in mystery. We knew that all kinds of special operations were carried out from there, but of what nature was left solely to the imagination.

Once the crews were safely on their way I sat back and carried on with the normal routine work, expecting to see them back in the course of a few days. The first intimation I had that something had in fact happened was when Joe McCarthy landed back at base a few days later. He came into my office quietly, and dumped a couple of kit bags on the floor.

'Weeden's and Bull's kit,' he said. 'They've had it.'

'Had it, Joe? When?'

'Last night. We operated on a special low-level attack. Dropping arms and ammunition. They must have hit trouble.' He added disgustedly, 'I didn't even find the bloody target area.'

Just as he said this, Sergeant Heveron came in from the orderly room, and handed me a couple of signals. He began to say 'Weeden......' I nodded,

'Alright Sergeant, I know.' On seeing McCarthy the sergeant realized my source of information.

'Shall I carry out the usual procedure sir?'

'Yes please,' I nodded.

Joe carried on where he had left off. 'I have got to go back to Tempsford,' he said. 'The remaining two of us may have to finish the job. Where's the CO?'

I told him that I thought he was in the operations room.

'OK. I'll push off and tell him. The other boys have the remainder of the kit. S'long Adj., see you in a day or two......perhaps.'

With that Joe had gone. As it happened, he came back, as did Clayton. The operation was ruled out because of certain conditions known only to those at the top.

The loss of Weeden and Bull on this particular job made me think more than ever how a bomber crews' life depended on the flip of a coin. A short detachment for a few days ……… and finish. Anyone might be chosen.

I learnt later that on 10th December 1943 a plane took off from Tempsford at 8.35 pm. Its mission was an arms drop over Northern France. The aircraft was hit by flak at low altitude and crashed. There were no survivors, and this is believed to have been FO Weedon and his crew.

At 9.12 pm a second aircraft took off on the same mission. This aircraft was also hit by flak and crashed. Two airmen died. One evaded capture and the others ended up in a POW camp. I think this was WO Bull and his crew.

9   CHRISTMAS 1943

Towards the end of 1943, under the guidance and leadership of Wing Commander Cheshire, we began to gain confidence and feel more like the original 'Dam Busters'. Operations became more frequent and were generally on targets in French territory. Strangely enough the main grumble I heard was the lack of opposition from the enemy.

'Just like cross country flights' was one of the comments I heard. Funny people these air crew chaps!

We had our next casualties in December 1943. Unfortunately we had arranged a squadron party and dance in Boston on this particular night. All the boys had been looking forward to fun and games and many 'dates' had been made for this our first dance. Then we had the news that the AOC had deemed that it would be a nice evening to operate. I heard many caustic remarks, some unprintable. Many officers came to me and asked me to tell Mabel, Mary, Joan (if I saw them), that they would be working and unable to keep their engagements.

I was most disappointed, for the whole affair had been carefully planned. Special transport, in the form of buses and trains, was available, both to and from Boston. Beer would flow, and the inevitable buns were there to meet the equally inevitable demands of hungry airmen. I wanted to put the whole show off but the Wing Commander decided that we had better carry on, for after all there would be plenty of airmen off duty and their plans also had to be considered.

So we had our party, and the Town Hall, Boston was packed to the doors with a happy crowd. I don't think those present noticed anything wrong, but I felt disheartened when I looked around for signs of wings and half wings. There were actually only two aircrew members of 617 Squadron at this party, and after all, a Squadron party means ALL the Squadron.

Perhaps I was too fussy and expected a lot in the midst of a war. My wife was there with me that night and I am afraid she shared my misery. Something a few of us had planned for months was shattered within a matter of hours, at least shattered as far as I was concerned. I had planned that the Wing Commander would make a speech to all his men. There would be games, aircrew versus ground crew, and the aircrew were airborne somewhere over France.

Then came the news next morning that we had lost a crew – Jeff Rice and his boys. Rice had recently been decorated for his gallant attack on the Dortmund Ems Canal. As I walked to my office in the cold December weather, thinking of this crew, the previous evening seemed an even worse flop. The attack hadn't been much good, the party hadn't been much good, the weather was bloody awful, and I wished I was back home in 'civvy street'. I had always had these feelings, but they didn't last long. One unfortunately became hardened.

Jeff Rice was subsequently reported captured but his crew were not so lucky and occupy a small tract of land in Germany. It is so important to remember these graves and all that they mean.

The final event of 1943, our year of formation, was of course Christmas, even if there was a war on. At Coningsby it was decided that the officers would devote their day to the airmen and WAAFs. Our party and dinner were to be on Boxing Day. A Christmas day in the RAF is something to remember. It's not like being at home of course, but the atmosphere on a really happy RAF station is really grand. On this particular day the weather was too bad for operations and consequently everyone could relax and forget the war for the moment.

The day started off with a breakfast enjoyed only by those who didn't enjoy the previous evening too much. The festivities were a great success. We served dinner to the Officer's Mess staff, and the airmen and WAAFs thoroughly enjoyed the occasion. Large jugs of beer were constantly emptied and replenished, and an impromptu dance was soon in full swing. A couple of the officers, led by Flight Lieutenant Jordan, had a bicycle race round the dining room, dressed in weird costumes, ranging from WAAF uniforms to football shorts worn with short socks, and oversized boots. Songs were sung, speeches were made, and each and everyone thought what a good fellow his or her immediate companion was.

Like all good things it had to come to an end, for after the beer had all gone, and the food had disappeared the party began to break up quietly, people drifting off to sleep away the effects of it all – the usual finish to an Air Force party. They always seemed to be like that to me. Plenty of fun and excitement for a long enough period, and then suddenly it was all over, and quiet prevailed.

On Boxing Day we had our official dinner in the Mess and although this was a pleasant enough affair, there was not much hair let down for we had one or two high-ranking personalities as guests, and the evening did not develop into a 'party'. Polite conversation and gentle laughter was the rule. Formal handshakes and good-byes brought the day to a close, and I personally had the feeling that although we had all been very reserved, with our usual high spirits in low gear, it was very nice to think that we could really be Officers and Gentlemen in the best traditions of the service.

After Boxing Day the year seemed to speed to its close, and little of note occurred.

The year 1943 had been one of mixed fortune, outstanding success on the one hand and bitter tragedy on the other. A Squadron had been born and had cut its teeth on the Ruhr dams. Fate had been reasonably kind on this occasion, and I say 'reasonably' because it can never be forgotten how many aircrew lost their lives on this magnificent operation. If Fate was with us in May 1943, she certainly deserted the Squadron in September, and reduced us to a fraction of our original number. We had enjoyed a period of convalescence, and had made a good recovery. We were now enjoying perfect health. A VC had been awarded, DSOs and DFCs, CGMs and DFMs had come our way. Our first Commanding Officer had already been superseded and 1944 loomed ahead. The one hope in the hearts of all was the end of the war, but as that event would be governed by many factors, it did not do to become too excited at the thought. The enemy was still very strong, but we knew we were getting stronger, and with that thought we were quietly confident of the outcome.

10 WOODHALL SPA

The first operation of any importance in 1944 was not a flying operation, but the move of the Squadron once again to new quarters. I suppose that the powers that be had some reason for these moves but it sometimes seemed absolutely futile to move a complete unit lock, stock and barrel a matter of a few miles. The work involved was colossal, and practically reduced those occupied in the staff jobs to physical and mental wrecks. The transportation of roughly one thousand men, plus aircraft, kit, bombs, motor vehicles, records, etc. etc. from A to B is obviously difficult and even though it was our second change of quarters I did not relish the task ahead.

The scenes on a station in the throes of the departure of a Bomber Squadron is a mixture of a race meeting, a crowd at a rugby match, and the London Underground in rush hour. Everyone seems to be going in different directions and there are times when it appears to be virtually impossible that order could possibly come out of the chaos.

Of course, even with the organisation the Royal Air Force had at its disposal, there were hitches, and tempers occasionally became a trifle frayed, but when you eventually counted up, by some miracle all was well.

The most interesting feature of a Squadron move was the rumours passed on to the outgoing personnel to the incoming, and vice versa. Concentration camps were mentioned in some instances, and from other sections one would be inclined to think that the new station was a form of pleasure resort. Station Commanders were discussed at high and low level. The most sensible attitude was to go ahead and find out for yourself.

The order to the aircrew was that they should take to the air unobtrusively and proceed according to all flying regulations to their new quarters. Something went slightly awry here, for although one or two of the lads 'stooged' away after take-off, quite a few seemed loath to leave the old homestead, and spent a few happy minutes flying their Lancasters past the control tower, just over the hangars, and in general 'beat up' the Station to the best of their ability. It was a good best too, and all of us on the ground enjoyed a spectacular display resembling pre-war Hendon until the CO stepped in and told the planes to proceed as ordered before they did any damage. The fun stopped, and the move went ahead according to plan. Incidentally, low flying is prohibited, and offenders are subject to disciplinary action, and although this may seem strict to some people, it is a very essential ruling. Valuable aircraft and lives can be, and in fact have been, lost due to chaps who have endeavoured to show off once too often. It may be asked 'how did they get away with it on this occasion?' I can only say that there are times when even the Royal Air Force has to be diplomatic!

For a day or two we were in the throes of settling down in our new quarters at RAF Station Woodhall Spa. Eventually order came and it seemed as though we had been there for years, and we sat back after the initial excitement to await the next operational orders from Group. They came steadily, and we were given some very special tasks which, although not arduous from the operational viewpoint, were exceptionally important to the Allied war effort. The majority of our targets were small factories in enemy occupied France, factories producing vital war materials. One of the most successful was an attack on the Gnome-Rhône Aero works at Limoges, led by Wing Commander Cheshire. A new low level marker technique was recommended by the Wing Commander for this operation. On this occasion he flew a Mosquito carrying the marker bombs and virtually placed them on the factory. The main force of the Squadron flying above, including the old guard of McCarthy, Shannon, Munro and Martin, dropped their bombs with such accuracy that the target was virtually obliterated. The Wing Commander reported that he could see the factory workpeople taking cover in the light of the flare, and our crews gave the Frenchmen a little time to get away before they carefully planted their 'cookies'.

The photographic reconnaissance proved that the raid had been so accurately fulfilled as to border on the uncanny. As a matter of fact senior American officers came down to the station to study our methods, and to congratulate 617 on their amazing work. It is all the more unbelievable when one realises that the bombing was carried out at night-time, and that the planes achieved these results from a height exceeding two miles.

It also seemed amazing to me that Wing Commander Cheshire could step out of a Lancaster aircraft, and take the lead in the Mosquito, a machine virtually new to him. Personally, I grope if I drive a new car, never mind an aeroplane.

The tail of the Squadron was now virtually 'up', and all connected with our new trail of 'scalps' felt frightfully bucked. We were the pride of Bomber Command (I know many will disagree here!) and our stock was never higher.

In between operations, it was not all sitting down and awaiting the next. The Squadron Commander had the aircraft practice bombing at every conceivable occasion, night and day, endeavouring to eliminate any possible errors. There were times when crews became 'browned off' with persistent cross country flying, and this bombing range warfare, but there is no doubt whatsoever that it paid amazing dividends. To keep morale as high as possible sweepstakes were run, and the most efficient crew over a short period of time would win a small prize, which immediately would be handed over the respective mess bar to refresh the gallant losers!

The occasional party would inevitably take place, romances would bloom and fade, fellows would be posted, and although it would not be noticeable at the time, the original 617 Squadron as formed, began to whittle away. Disciplinary action of course, had to be taken at times, but on the whole we did not have many bad boys and those we did have were soon called to order.

The author with Squadron Leader 'Jock' Calder at Woodhall Spa, 1944

Casualties seemed to be a thing of the past, and we began to assume the mentality of a peace-time unit. Perhaps that is not true. I should say that I began to assume that outlook. On the 13th February 1944, fate took a hand again, and in that peculiar warped way, hit us hard without warning.

The Squadron was briefed to attack the Antheor Viaduct once again. This bridge in the South of France had withstood all our efforts, and seemed bombproof. This time we felt sure the job could be finished, and the operation was detailed to take off from a station in the south of England, to cut down on distance for petrol conservation. The leader again was Wing Commander Cheshire. In fact I should have to think very hard to find any occasion when he did not lead 617 whilst he was in command.

The enemy had become used to our periodic visits to the viaduct, and a hot reception awaited our crews. The Wingco tried to start the attack, but was driven off by intense anti-aircraft opposition. Our own inimitable 'Mick' Martin then went in, and ran the gauntlet of blazing guns. His own gunners blazed away furiously at the flack positions, and the aircraft shuddered and yawed dangerously as Bob Hay, the bomber leader, tried desperately to get the target in the bombsight. A particularly heavy burst under the nose of the Lancaster made Mick realise that he would have to disengage, and hugging the water as closely as possible he flew out to sea. The main force of the Squadron valiantly endeavoured to press home the attack, but on this occasion luck was out and the CO had to withdraw the Squadron, with the knowledge that if any damage had been caused it could only have been superficial.

What of 'Mick' Martin? Yes, he survived, but poor old Bob Hay, our bombing leader, was killed during the bombing run. It is impossible to record the feelings of the other members of the crew. They represented a team of Australians who had seen virtually all their operations together, and the father of them all, Bob, was dead. The aircraft landed in a battered condition in Sardinia, and I believe that the gallant Bob Hay still rests there. In a week or two Micky brought the machine back, still much the worse for wear. He silently handed me the odd one or two items Bob had taken with him, and told me there and then that he would now have to leave the Squadron. It seemed an unbelievable decision, but he meant it. The funny thing was that he left us to become a night fighter pilot, for a rest he said. Some fellows have a peculiar idea of rest! The remainder of his crew went to non-operational posts, for they had finished their tour of duty as operational aircrew, and I believe most of them were eventually repatriated to Australia not long afterwards.

This was not the end of our bad luck on the 13th. On the return of the Squadron from the advance base, one of our Flight Commanders, Squadron Leader Bill Suggitt, flew into the side of a hill, and all excepting Bill himself died instantly. Another Squadron Leader Tommy Lloyd, the Station Intelligence Officer, was also coming back in this machine, and he too perished in the crash. Squadron Leader Suggitt died from his injuries a few hours after the accident. From a few peaceful weeks without any casualties, they came all at once, but ironically enough they came on our own doorstep. I always felt it was so much worse in instances like this. When the lads did not return from a trip there was always a chance, but this type of thing was so final. They were dead, no further hope at all. The majority of this crew being Dominion personnel, we buried them with full military honours in the local churchyard.

Reverting back to the point of feeling it so much more when men were killed when not actually operating, I always found that I began on such occasions to think more about the men involved, than I did when they were just reported 'missing'. I suppose it is something like reading about a train crash in the papers, when numerous people are injured, or even killed, and getting a sudden feeling of sympathy which passes, and yet feeling horrified if your next door neighbour dies of natural causes.

Take Suggitt for instance. He reminded me of a sort of morose James Stewart. He was tall, thin and gangling, with apparently little taste for anything other than reading books of a classical nature. He did not drink or smoke, and always retired to bed early, usually with some caustic remarks about the members of the mess who stayed behind indulging in their favourite occupation of beer drinking. It cannot be said that Bill was popular in the mess, but that was really his own fault, for he just made no attempt to fraternise. Even his own crew found him difficult at times, for he generally treated them in rather a condescending manner. In fact, he made the decisions as the Captain, in a manner similar to a schoolteacher addressing his pupils. As a pilot however, his ability could not be questioned, neither could his courage. He could throw a Lancaster around as if it was a child's toy, and for the courage part he had a DFC ribbon to show. A strange bloke, but then it takes all kinds to make a world, or a Bomber Squadron.

Now Tommy Lloyd, the Station Intelligence Officer, was the opposite, the exact opposite to Suggitt. He was bright, breezy, and made everyone feel as if they were personal friends of his. He threw parties, stood all the expense, took his drink like a gentleman, and yet still found time to work more hours than necessary. Ribbons showed that he had taken part in the 1914–18 'rumpus', and although he was practically twice my age, he had a zest for life that would have done credit to a teenager. He only went on the operation which cost his life as an observer, to give him first hand knowledge for his job of work. More's the tragedy that he saw what he wanted, but didn't live to use the information.

The next few weeks saw the intensification of bombing attacks against enemy installations, which we know now as the prelude to the invasion of Europe. The Germans were attacked day and night, without respite, and while the main force of Bomber Command carried out the usual saturation raids on the German cities, our boys were detailed to eliminate small specially selected targets, generally in enemy occupied territory. Wing Commander Cheshire evolved a new marker technique of literally placing a marker flare on the target, by using a fast aircraft flying at low level. In his case the Mosquito was the chosen machine.

The Lancasters following up achieved outstanding success, and the majority of the targets were virtually obliterated. One of the most outstanding operations of this series was against the Gnome-Rhône Aero works in France, which was most severely damaged. Considering that this was a single factory, and a night operation, I must be forgiven if I brag a little at the prowess of 617 Squadron. Only twelve aircraft operated, and nine of these produced a photograph of the aiming point! I was not an operational type, but it must have been good, for high ranking American Air Force Officers came down to the station, not only to congratulate the boys, but to find out how it was done. The Gnome-Rhône effort was carried out in February 1944, and as far as we were concerned was really the highlight of the month. In March there was no slackening of the tempo, and although the aircrew boys were thoroughly enjoying themselves, they seemed to be spending most of their time either flying or sleeping. The beer consumption during the early part of 1944 must have slackened off considerably.

A postcard from a POW Camp.

It reads:

Monday May 22nd / 44

Dear Humphreys, A line to let you know we decided to spend our seven days leave over here but cannot promise when we shall be back. Camp life is pretty good thanks to the Red Cross; plenty of sport and everyone looking very fit and sun-burned. My regards to all and best of luck; tell the boys to keep it up.   *Jim Cooper*

11   THE *TIRPITZ* RAID

In September 1944 UK and Soviet forces combined in Operation 'Paravane' which was launched against the German battleship, *Tirpitz*, which was anchored in the Norwegian Alten Fjord. The *Tirpitz* had been successfully attacking northern convoys and although it had been damaged several times it was still posing a danger for merchant convoys sailing to Murmansk and Arkhangel in the Russian north.

The Russians had made a number of attempts to sink the battleship but their available bombers were not capable of carrying bombs sufficiently powerful to do the job so Lancasters from No. 9 and No. 617 squadrons were drafted in.

The attack was led by Wing Commander 'Willie' Tait and comprised eighteen aircraft from No. 9 Squadron, twenty from 617, a Lancaster from No. 463 Squadron (Australian) and a crew from No. 5 Group Film Unit. Twenty-four Lancasters carried the 'Tallboy' bomb, the others had 'Jonnie Walker' mines. They took off on 11th September from Lossiemouth and all went well for the first five hours, though one Lancaster from No. 9 Squadron had to return to base as its bomb had become loose and had to be jettisoned. They flew 2,000 miles to Arkhangel where they refuelled before flying a further 600 miles to the target in Alten Fjord. Early on 12th September, on reaching Russian territory, the planes began to land at various airports. Thirteen Lancasters did not reach their designated airfields and seven were damaged on landing.

On 15th September 1944 twenty-seven Lancasters attacked the *Tirpitz*. Only one of the twenty-one 'Tallboy' bombs was a direct hit and the *Tirpitz* survived, though damaged to such an extent that full repairs could only be carried out at one of the German naval bases. Her fate had been sealed. All the planes returned safely to Yagodnik airfield and over the next twelve days flew back to England – a round trip of over 5,000 miles.

Six Lancasters stayed on Russian soil after the mission, apparently they were deemed write-offs. Later two planes were back in the air, with Soviet Air Force red stars on the fuselage and wings. The armament was removed and wrecked noses were replaced by transparent blisters. They were used on anti-submarine patrols, ice reconnaissance and transport duties. After the war one plane went to Riga Aviation College and was used for training, the other broke itself landing at Moscow and could not be repaired.

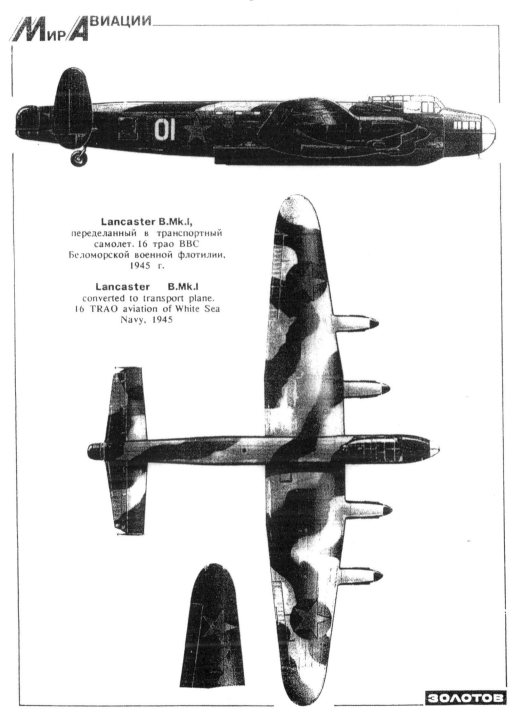

МирАвиации

Lancaster B.Mk.I,
переделанный в транспортный
самолет. 16 трао ВВС
Беломорской военной флотилии,
1945 г.

Lancaster   B.Mk.I
converted to transport plane.
16 TRAO aviation of White Sea
Navy, 1945

ЗОЛОТОВ

12   AFTERMATH

The story written up to this point was started after I was demobilized from the Royal Air Force, and the reason for not completing the memoirs up to the end of 617 Squadron's operational record during wartime was due entirely to the knowledge that Paul Brickhill had been commissioned to write the 'Dam Busters' story. As he was a recognised professional writer my version was unlikely to be accepted by a publisher.

I, as the Adjutant of the Squadron, had lived with the flying men and known them as comrades. Brickhill had to get his information from official sources and contact with surviving airmen, to put together his version.

He wrote to me, stating that he understood that I had maintained my own diaries of the work of the Squadron and he would appreciate access to them. I was not pleased to hand over information that I had devoted so much time and effort to, and frankly said so. I was in fact not very helpful, feeling that my story was mine!

Eventually Leonard Cheshire, the second commander I served under, intervened. He put it to me that the Brickhill version would go ahead with or without my co-operation, and he'd be most appreciative if I handed my stuff over. He was a man I could never oppose, so Brickhill got the material, which I must say, he used to good purpose.

Leonard Cheshire, the late Lord Cheshire VC, DSO, DFC was of course an Air Force legend and the founder of the well-known Cheshire Homes.

The *Dambusters* film based on Brickhill's book was accepted by the surviving crews – and myself – as a fair representation of 617 Squadron and the famous raid.

That, therefore, explains why I did not complete my own rather more personal version of the Dambusters, from foundation of the Squadron to the time I was posted overseas in the spring of 1945. What actually happened in the way of operational activity is adequately covered by Brickhill and other official versions. From my point of view the highlights were the tremendous success of the Barnes Wallis 'Tallboy', a 12,000 lb. armour-piercing bomb being dropped with amazing precision on submarine pens and rocket sites, and destroying Hitler's secret weaponry which would have been aimed at London. All the attacks were led by Cheshire, now flying a Mustang to mark the targets, which culminated in the award of the Victoria Cross for continuous conspicuous gallantry. Then sadly he left the Squadron on the orders of the top Air Force commanders, who considered he had done his share. He had flown nearly 100 operational flights and it was to be a desk for him, which he hated. I later received letters from him from Washington and India.

His command was taken over by Wing Commander J. B. Tait, DSO, DFC, a completely different personality altogether, but after being carefully 'vetted' by the aircrews, he soon got into the swing of things, and once again we had a brave and popular leader. He carried on with the Mustang, and the 'Tallboy' attacks continued unabated.

We then had 617 dropping 'window' over the English Channel to delude the German radar into thinking that a naval force was where it wasn't at the time of the D-day landings.

The highlight of 1944 was the successful attack on the *Tirpitz* and the sinking of the battleship, with the support of No. 9 Squadron. Not long after this the AOC decided that Tait had to stand down from ops after gaining four DSOs and two DFCs which I believe is a record. The Squadron now bore no resemblance to the original. Surviving Dambusters had departed to other fields, either to become trainers or, in the case of many overseas personnel, going home to finish out the war.

The next commander of 617 was a Canadian, Group Captain Johnnie Fauquier, DSO, DFC, who had volunteered his services, dropping down from a much higher rank to do so. He was much older than the normal aircrew, and myself, who at that time was the ripe old age of twenty-nine. He was not the normal Squadron Commander 617 had been used to. He was tough talking to the point of rudeness at times, but he did what his predecessors had done – he led from the front.

Then came the 'Grand Slam' bomb from the Barnes Wallis stable, a ten-ton effort. This was used to devastating effect against bridges and the like, cutting off the retreat of German troops and really, from this point, the end of the war was in sight.

I seemed to have served my purpose too and was posted overseas to the Japanese theatre, arriving in Bombay on 8th May, VE Day, and incidentally my birthday. I was not amused and it was another year before I was eventually released after an undistinguished period of activity.

Then back home to family and 'civvy' life, and eventually to start my book on the 617. During the peace we all met from time to time, often at reunions, and a monument was erected at Woodhall Spa in Lincolnshire in tribute to the 'Dambusters'. Sadly now there are only a few of the 'originals' left, and I am writing these words now to put them on record before I too have to leave the scene.

Over the years I had collected a vast scrapbook of memorabilia and when this was auctioned at Bonham's in London in May 1996 the event created great interest. There was national press coverage and I appeared on Anglia Television and spoke on the BBC Today programme and on local radio. Grantham in Lincolnshire was the 617 Squadron GQ so in effect the material was 'going home'. There was a public presentation in November 1996 and it is still on display in Grantham Museum.

13   OFFICERS COMMANDING

It occurred to me even after I had stopped writing my version of the 'Dambusters' that there were other things I could call to mind which would probably be of interest – more personal observations not covered in the mainly operational offerings of others.

WING COMMANDER GUY GIBSON, VC DSO, DFC

Guy Gibson is of course the first who comes to mind. One of the most disappointing occasions, during my very short association with him, happened just after the raid on the dams when the remainder of the Squadron was on leave. We had to stay behind because of casualty procedures. Much to my delight he suggested that we should have our photograph taken in front of Lancaster 'G' for George, his own machine. We enlisted the aid of the photographic section, and duly posed. Much to my dismay and disappointment the pictures did not turn out. We did not get another chance so I lost the opportunity of a wonderful souvenir.

There was an occasion when Gibson and several other members of the squadron went to a theatre in Lincoln, and the spotlight flitted to and fro as the chorus girls danced. Supposedly this was seized upon by the Wing Commander as the answer to the problem of flying a Lancaster at very low level over the dams, and the spotlight altimeter was born. This was a process whereby a fixed light was put onto each wing of the aircraft, and when they converged, the plane was held steady for the bombing run. I believe this was a bit of dramatic licence (in the film version) and that it was actually the brainchild of the backroom boys.

The image of Guy Gibson forever imprinted in my mind during our really short relationship was that of a born leader, in the highest tradition of the services. He was sometimes intolerant but he had no self-doubts as to his mission, and he had a manner that instilled positive attitudes in the minds of those under his command. He was special, and had he survived, I am sure he would have reached the top in the RAF. He was killed in action on 19th September 1944, leading a main force raid after choosing to continue ops when he could have taken a desk job. His wife, Eve, subsequently re-married, in 1948, to Jack Hyman and lived in South Africa. This marriage did not last and I understand Eve reverted to the surname Gibson. She has also passed on.

WING COMMANDER LEONARD CHESHIRE, VC, DSO, DFC

The Wing Commander dropped rank to join 617 Squadron. 'Chesh', as he was to his intimates, was the opposite of Guy Gibson. Scholarly in manner, slim of build and most elegant as he strolled about his work. I never saw him rush about as many of us were wont to do during periods of operational activities yet at the back of this calm exterior his brain must have been an engine room of superb quality. He also had a wicked sense of humour and I have seen him 'send up' the top brass with an absolutely straight face. I had at times been on the receiving end of his humour. He occasionally came up with ideas that bordered on the edge of fantasy.

I remember he once suggested to the top brass that for Christmas 1943 we should mount an operation, with Lancasters dropping Christmas parcels on German POW camps. This was turned down by Bomber Command. Most of his operational ideas, however, were used to our advantage.

One of his greatest achievements was the foundation of the Cheshire Homes, now one of the greatest charity successes ever. His original idea of self-supporting units for ex-service personnel unfortunately failed, and many who joined him on this project lost their money. I recall one of them, Gumley Hall near Market Harborough in Leicestershire, could not continue and had to close. As a matter of a fact he had earlier approached me on this matter to see if I was interested. As I had a young family to support, and a mortgage after returning to my civilian occupation, I reluctantly declined, as, I believe, did other members of the wartime squadron.

After quite a lot of hardship health wise, he eventually started the Cheshire Homes, and the rest is history. He married Sue Ryder, also a famous name in the charity world, and converted to Roman Catholicism. They had two children. Lady Ryder and Lord Cheshire have now sadly passed on, but have left behind a wonderful legacy to the nation.

Lord Cheshire had been previously married, to an American, Constance Binney, a 'showbiz' celebrity. This marriage was really doomed from the very beginning. I met Constance at Woodhall Spa, at an officer's mess dance, when she came over from the United States. My wife had travelled from Leicester for the occasion. Both of us, to put it mildly, were amazed when we were introduced to Constance. I had seen a photograph of her in the Wing Commander's room. She had a beautiful film star face but she looked, and no doubt was, many years his senior. To me it seemed a most unlikely relationship. I do not really know how it all ended but she went back to the States, and 'Ches' stayed home. Eventually that arrangement became permanent and the parting official.

I have not mentioned the award of the Victoria Cross to Leonard Cheshire. It is not generally known that the original citation for an award for continuous gallantry recommended a further bar to his DSO. When this was presented to higher authority, they considered that the VC was the appropriate award, and how right they were!

SQUADRON LEADER MICK MARTIN, DSO, DFC

H. B. 'Mick' Martin was a one off, an extrovert. I met him officially at RAF Skellingthorpe, near Lincoln, when I was working as a supernumerary Pilot Officer with 50 Squadron, standing in for the Squadron Adjutant. He came to 617 as a volunteer, and was then made a Flight Lieutenant. He was a master pilot, even then on the way to becoming a legend. He always carried a Koala bear as his mascot when operating (he was an Aussie, as were his crew). He was destined for greatness, but succeeded beyond my wildest dreams, retiring as Air Vice Marshall Sir Harold Martin, CBE, DSO, DFC. To think what a tear-about he was in his Dam Buster days!

The last time I saw him was, I think, at a reunion at Woodhall Spa when the memorial to 'The Dambusters' was unveiled. He looked frail at that time, and did not participate in the speeches. He had unfortunately been involved earlier in a road accident, from which he never really recovered. He died a few years ago.

WING COMMANDER J. B. 'WILLIE' TAIT, DSO, DFC

Although 'Willie' Tait had a hard act to follow after Guy Gibson and Leonard Cheshire, he did not let the side down. I really believe his collection of four DSOs could well have been another VC for 617 Squadron. It must have been a close thing and I have often wondered if the fact that the first two commanding officers gained that award could have affected the final decision.

The highlight of Willie Tait's operational career must have been the sinking of the battleship *Tirpitz* in November 1944, when 617 Squadron and 9 Squadron finally administered the *coup de grace*, using Barnes Wallis's 12,000 'Tallboy' bomb. Shortly after this attack the Wing Commander flew to London in a Lancaster, taking his entire crew, and me, with him. He scrawled his version of the attack on the pages of an exercise book (in pencil) and broadcast this on the BBC.

Presumably he took us along for moral support, and afterwards he invited us all

Guy Gibson

Leonard Cheshire

Sir Ralph Cochrane

J. B. Tait

J. E. Fauquier

to dinner at the Mayfair Hotel. His wife-to-be, Betty Plummer, was present. His pencilled notes I retained, and they are held in the Dambuster collection at Grantham Museum in Lincolnshire. He retired a Group Captain, and keeps a low profile. I understand that he has lost his wife. He remains Life President of the 617 Squadron Association.

GROUP CAPTAIN FAUQUIER, DSO, DFC

I do not remember too much of his era as the RAF posted me away whilst he was in command. There was, however, one particular operation I remember, the attack on enemy shipping in the Bergen region of Norway, on 12th January 1945. This seemed to be a fairly routine attack, but unfortunately it turned out to be one of our 'bad' days.

Flight Lieutenant John Prior was shot down but survived and he and his crew were taken prisoner. The most tragic accident was the loss of Flying Officer Ian Ross and his entire crew. They ditched in the sea and were last seen alive on the wing of the aircraft. Air Sea Rescue managed to drop a dinghy in the vicinity and it was reported that the airmen were seen to be trying to swim to it. The rescue aircraft had to leave the scene because of fighter activity and it was assumed they would be taken prisoner. Ross's crew were never found, or reported by the Germans or Norwegians. One theory is that they could have been strafed by a fighter, or they could have drowned as it would have been bitterly cold. Tom Bennett who reported this operation in his book said that how the crew perished remains unsolved, but to ditch safely and then lose their lives was a tragedy.

I left 617 Squadron soon after this operation, but in effect the war was practically over in Europe.

GERRY WITHERICK, DFC, DFM

An air gunner extraordinaire, Gerry had over 100 sorties as a gunner, when he was recommended for a DFC. The powers above asked 'Had there been any operational incidents in his career?' Leonard Cheshire who originated the citation said

'A hundred sorties against the enemy – operational incidents?!!'

Gerry got his medal. He finished up running a pub in Tooley Street in London on demob. but to me the word hero applies to this fearless airman. He was actually shot down on one of the attacks on the *Tirpitz* and his pilot crash landed in Sweden. He sent me a letter from the Astoria Hotel in Stockholm. When he came back he just resumed operations. Quite a man!

FLIGHT LIEUTENANT DAVE SHANNON, DSO, DFC

He was an original 'Dambuster' and also one of the few survivors on the ill-fated Dortmund Ems canal raid in September 1943. He carried on under Leonard Cheshire until he too was told to 'call it a day' operationally. Although an Australian, he chose to stay in England and married a WAAF officer, Anne Fowler. They used to send me a card each Christmas, usually a print of one of Anne's drawings. She fought cancer, but eventually lost the battle. David was devastated and sadly he too died not long after. He was a wonderful pilot and was adored by his crew.

SQUADRON LEADER JOE McCARTHY, DSO, DFC

Another original 'Dambuster' and an American in the Royal Air Force. He was a massive hunk of a man physically, but really a gentle giant. He was also under Cheshire's command for a while. He stayed in the forces after the war and I believe he was a Wing Commander in the Royal Canadian Air Force until retirement. Originally he was a lifeguard in civilian life and a great swimmer. He used to enjoy ducking me in our local baths in Lincoln, outdoors in those days! He also passed on not very long ago. He seemed indestructible.

SQUADRON LEADER GEORGE HOLDEN, DSO, DFC

George Holden was posted to 617 Squadron to take over from Guy Gibson. He led the attack on the Dortmund Ems canal. He had expected to take over Guy Gibson's crew, but not all joined him. The flight engineer in Gibson's crew, a Flight Sergeant Pulford, was for some reason not accepted by Holden and was dropped to become a spare. Flight Lieutenant Trevor-Roper, the rear gunner decided he would now prefer to take his operational rest period. Leaving Gibson's crew did not however save their lives. Pulford became an engineer to Squadron Leader Suggitt and perished when he crashed, and Trevor-Roper came back to operations with another squadron, and was killed in action. As a matter of interest I met George Holden's sister at the 50th Anniversary reunion.

So, none of Guy Gibson's crew survived the war, and George Holden never became a Wing Commander. The toll of Bomber Command.

14   HEROES ALL

These afterthoughts would not be complete without reference to other aircrew of 617 Squadron – a few who flew on 16th May and survived the raid, and so many who were not actual 'Dambusters' but who nevertheless flew with distinction on many important targets after the 'main event'.

For example, Wing Commander Cheshire and Wing Commander Tait did not participate in the dams attack, neither did Gerry Witherick or George Holden, but they were of course equal in their skill and bravery.

There are so many post dam-raid aircrew I recall:

SqnLdr 'Tony' Iveson, DFC	FltLt 'Terry' Kearns, DFC
FltLt 'Danny' Daniels, DFC	FltLt Keith Astbury, DFC
FltLt 'Bob' Knights, DSO, DFC	
Captain 'Nicky' Knilans, DSO, DFC, an American	
FltLt Pat Kelly, DFC	Pilot Officer Jock Chalmers, DFC
SqnLdr 'Jock' Calder, DSO, DFC	Pilot Officer 'Spam' Spafford, DFC
FltLt John Pryor	FltLt Ralph Allsebrook, DFC
FltLt Duffy, DFC	SqnLdr 'Gerry' Fawke, DSO, DFC

These readily come to mind, but there are many others. It would take another journal to recall all those worthy of mention so I have to ask forgiveness for this, but so many years have passed since I was a young man and age brings its limitations. Some of the above died on operations, some of natural causes, and a few are still around. Whatever the case they are all brave men.

15   CORRESPONDENCE

About a year after he left I had a letter from Guy Gibson. It was short – he did not like paperwork – but it is the only personal letter I ever had from him. It was sent from RAF Staff College, Gerrard's Cross and read

14.4.44

My dear Humph,

   Hope a lot of the old faces are still going strong. Awfully sorry to hear about Bob Hay and Tommy Lloyd.

   I wonder if you could have a look around for my old personal file. In it there might be a report I once wrote on the Le Creusot Raid.

   I don't mean personal letters, I meant operations.

This is a wizard joint – like fuck

Ever All Boy   Guy Gibson

The contents of this letter do show that he disliked paper work. Bob Hay was killed on operations and Squadron Leader Lloyd died when his plane crashed, returning to base.

   Leonard Cheshire was a more forthcoming correspondent and I had a number of letters from him after he was moved on. From HQ, Eastern Air Command, South East Asia, he wrote in 1944

Wed 25th

My dear Adj.,

   Will you pass on to everyone my sincerest and warmest congratulations on all their magnificent exploits. It is a long way from your war out here, and it's difficult to get exact news of what you are doing. None the less I have heard enough to know that the hardest and the greatest Air Fighting is being done by you, and I take pains to see to it that people out here realise it.

15.4.44.

My Dear Humph.

Hope a lot of the old faces are still going strong. Awfully sorry to hear about Bob Hay. And Tommy Lloyd.

I wonder if you could have a look around for my old personal file. In it there might be a report I once wrote on the Le Creusot Raid.

I don't mean personal letters – I meant operations.

This is a wizard joint – like fuck.

Ever All Best. Guy P. Gibson

The only letter I have from Guy Gibson

I play a very minor part in events, sitting in a chair writing memoranda, reports and other works of art suitable for the waste paper basket, and occasionally do my rounds in an old Hurricane.

I would give a great deal to call in on the old office and have Cpl. Munro or Wakeman fetch in a cup of tea.

My kindest regards to everyone (including yourself) and tell them I'll prepare a suitable reception should they ever come out here.

Yours most sincerely,
Leonard Cheshire

In February 1944 he wrote from Washington where he had obviously been in hospital.

Feb 2nd
British Joint Staff Mission

Public Health Building
Washington, DC

My Dear Adj.

Through a chain of somewhat complicated circumstances I have fetched up in this country more or less for keeps. I am so sorry for the single reason that I thoroughly enjoyed my job in India and was not very far away from the front line. I succeeded in getting 2 ops in an old Com flight aeroplane, by the simple process of accidentally setting red on blue. I'd hardly call it a hazardous operation – the only obstacle being trees. At the moment I'm convalescing at a place called Balboa on the Californian coast. I expect to get back to Washington in a fortnight.

My purpose in writing is first to greet you, second to tell you – and most sincerely I can assure you – that I'd give anything to be back at Petwood, and third to ask you to do something for me. I have lost all contact with England, and since leaving the country have been living in a totally different world to the one you and I knew at Petwood. I've had to resign myself to the different life, but I can't resign myself to losing all touch with the old 617. I read today in the Los Angeles Times that Gibby's death had been confirmed. Why the hell they let him fly I can't think, Damn them. That seems to leave no-one but Micky, Dave, Mack and Les. Will you be good enough, Adj., to keep in touch with them all for me, and let me know from time to time where they are, and what they're doing? Aside from the memory of old times, I badly want to see them before we all break up and go our various ways about the world. By 'them' I mean anyone who talks our language. I've been thinking quite a bit about the future and have a proposition to offer, I think it's a good one, but I want to talk it over with you first and see what you've got to say. So if you can keep a link going somehow, that will be just dandy (American slang).

I wrote to Les from Delhi telling him I thought we were all set to hit the road again. Well, so we were, in fact it was all but fixed when someone went and pulled a fast one on me and I found myself here. I feel quite guilty because I must have disturbed his peace of mind, but I couldn't do anything about it because for 9 weeks I wasn't able to communicate with the outside world at all. I hope he's not too mad at me.

I don't know whether you're still at Petwood, or if you are who's still there with you, but I hope to know all about it when I get your answer. If you are there my very best wishes to everyone, including Simon.

This isn't a very good letter, but you know what I'm getting at. Also my very best wishes to Mrs Adj.

Yours ever,
Leonard Cheshire

P.S. I've a suspicion my belongings that were to've been sent from Petwood to my home have gone astray. Can you possibly initiate enquiries?

The proposition he indicates he would like to put to not only me but to some of his ex-pilots was a scheme to start self-contained communities, carrying on service comradeship.

I had been posted to Kandy, in Ceylon and from British Joint Staff Mission in Washington I received a letter dated 25 May 1945.

My dear Humph:-
Thank you so much for your letter but I am very sorry to hear the news it contained. This is just a short note to send you all my best wishes and my hopes that you won't be out there too long.

Things are a little rushed right now but I will write you more fully later on. If I cannot organise anything for you now, I still have something pretty good up my sleeve for the future for you.

With all best wishes,
Yours ever,
Chesh

At about the same time I had a series of letters from Willie Tait, writing from East Dereham in Norfolk.

31 May [1945]

My dear Humph

It was a shock to find you had disappeared so quickly and you went before I knew you were even going. I think that you have the great consolation though that it won't be for so long now. Everything seems to be moving very quickly towards the conclusion, so maybe the snakes and mosquitoes will be pro-British by the time you get there! After your healthful sea voyage you must be indecently bronzed and fit like a Nazi Youth Leader. Strength through Humphries. Farewell to Woodhall! Still it was good while it lasted.

In the comparative relaxation afterwards one can let the old brain settle. I am reading all the books I have had lying idle so long, and plan the post war Air Force. If there is any break at all between this war and the next! The situation in Europe is too touchy even to talk about.

Betty has been in the clutches of the medicos for some weeks, but they have done their butchering now, and she will soon be up again, and better. Lying in the sun which has actually been shining, at Blackpool, has been good in itself after five years of primieval existence on various camps.

Micky Martin is here, vivant, and only slightly bowed down by the cares of the matrimonial state, but so burnished and smart he is known as Immaculate Martin.

Life is enlivened by a few aerial visits to familiar scenes of past days – but in different circumstances! I mean Germany. The desolation is indescribable. For once the newspapers do not lie. It is awe-inspiring, and melancholy. Rusty iron and rubble. Reaping the whirlwind!

But that was a long time ago, as far away as last week's drunk, but the headache lasts longer.

In the meantime here's to your quick return. I shall be glad to see you again.

Yours ever,

Willie Tait

I wrote back, giving him such news as I had and his reply came back some months later.

Bylaugh Hall
Dereham
Norfolk
1 Sept [1945]

Dear Humph

Many thanks for your explosive letter. It jumps about on the desk of its own accord! It must be the heat and snakes makes you so choleric! The war is over at last, and believe me there is nothing to do in this land. Some people are doing their best to prolong it in their imagination, if not in reality, but I suppose that will gradually die. In the meantime I am trying to occupy the days profitably studying history, Russian, economics, in strict rotation, and trying to laugh off all the magazine articles which say all Armies, Air Forces, and Navies are completely obsolete now and should be disbanded forthwith.

I have also done the Cranwell discip.course, to the mutual benefit of the instructors and myself. They said 'You're too clever by half' – glowering. Apparently when I gazed at the lecturers in rapt attention it put them off.

And having carefully taught me that one has a come back if a report is adverse, they didn't dare give me the chance. In points of dispute I stated that Humphries did it such and such a way and that was final, and you will have to answer any comebacks.

The country is depressingly lethargic at present, industries don't start because men aren't released, and men aren't released because industries haven't started. Prices of houses zoom ever upwards, and the Tait ménage looks like being half a Nissan hut.

I am going to Norway next week, which should be amusing if I don't get chased by a polar bear, or have some other dire catastrophe.

Tony Iveson is plying between here and Sydney. He writes periodically to say he has a wedding present in his keeping, but doesn't seem to progress far in handing it over. If you happen to intercept him ask him how we qualify.

Yours ever,
Willie Tait

In October Willie himself was posted to Delhi.

HQ 226 Group
RAF
South East Asia
13 November '45

My Dear Humph

I scribbled a line to you a few weeks ago to the address on your last letter, which was long obsolete, and which you will probably never get. It was only when I had been in

Kandy some weeks I looked you up in P2 and found you were on the strength of HQ ACSEA. But you never showed up while I was there, so are doubtless marooned in some monsoon girt swamp, or up a palm tree surrounded by cobras.

I came up here (Delhi) about a week ago and I am administering with some considerable velocity, and if you imagine I don't know anything about administration, just come and see. KRS, AMO's, ACSEA Admin ins. AFO's, AFI's India Acts – I just eat them. And you would be quite right.

I forget what your release group is but I expect you are about due to go home. Try and drop in here sometime on your wanderings if you can before you go. But if I don't see you – all the best of luck.

If you were here for a time or the AM accepted your extension of service which I know you will be keen to apply for I have got just the job for you.

As you will probably never get this I am not bothering to write any more until I hear from you.

Yours ever

    Willie Tait

16   PAUL BRICKHILL

In June1950 I received the following letter from Paul Brickhill.

Dear Mr Humphries

With the warm support of Air Chief Marshall Sir Ralph Cochrane I am prepar-ing to write the history of 617 squadron, and he, Micky Martin and others have given me your name as a man who knows most of the gen.

It is not to be a formal history, but more of the human story of the squadron. Sir Ralph is very keen that it should be a story of the RAF spirit, and I quite agree.

For that I want human details of the squadron, anecdotes, little sidelights on per-sonalities and the little, human inside details behind the formal activities. Also I want the ground crew side as well as the air-borne elements.

The bare bones of the history I already have. Now I need the inside. Domestic details. If you remember any little stories on these lines I'd be awfully grateful if you could find time to jot a few of them down; little things that people said or did and so on. If, by any chance, you happen to be coming to London soon we could meet and talk. These things come out so much more vividly in conversation.

Do please drop me a line if you think you might be able to help.

> *Very sincerely,*
> *Paul Brickhill*

My first reaction was of intense annoyance. When 617 was formed Guy Gibson asked me to take note of all that happened and some day to write the story of the squadron. I promised to do this, not as a terse official report but a story of the human side; of men living with the horror of war. I accumulated all the information I could and made notes of every colourful or interesting occasion. By the time Paul Brickhill wrote, I had some one hundred typewritten pages covering the Dam Raid, the Dortmund Ems Canal effort of September 1943 and details up to Christmas of that year.

I realised that Brickhill would not have been aware of my efforts but the thought of passing my 'gen' over was something I could not do. I did, rather unfairly, say that no prospective author likes to be robbed of his plot and also told him '…my days with 617 are something I shall never forget and if I ever complete my story at least I shall have lived it, but I will have no part in a "phony" history'.

His reply of 6th June 1950 said:

Dear Mr Humphries

Your letter was quite a surprise. I had no idea…that you were compiling a history of 617. In the circumstances let me make it clear that I am not asking you to hand your material over. I do not wish in any way to interfere with your 617 story.

Your suggestion that I am robbing you of your plot is not quite the case. I am a professional writer and have been for some time, and though writers are now naturally turning their attention to recording epic stories of the war, this book has been none of my seeking. I was approached to write it by the Vice Chief of the Air Staff, Air Chief Marshal the Hon. Sir Ralph Cochrane, and the whole thing has been arranged on a fairly high level.

It is a pity that the work should be duplicated but having promised to undertake the book and having done some preliminary groundwork I am in no position to withdraw. The Vice Chief would justifiably be very angry if I tried to.

…Your suggestion that mine will be a 'phony' history is not justified. I served six years in the Air Force during the war as an operational pilot and I know the atmosphere of Air Force Life and operations pretty well.

Also, Sir Ralph, Leonard Cheshire, Micky Martin and very many others are co-operating fully in supplying details of the squadron's career. Not knowing that you were compiling the story too I had hoped for your co-operation, but I quite understand your feeling that you would like to complete your own story.

I hope you will appreciate too that as an experienced writer and Ex-Air Force officer commissioned by the Vice Chief to write the story, I have equal justification to tackle it.

It is a pity that the two efforts should be so dispersed but I am afraid there is not much I can do about it.

Yours faithfully
Paul Brickhill

The next letter in this saga was a bit of a surprise.

Paul Brickhill

National Aeronautical Estab.
Thurleigh
Bedford,
June 27th

My Dear Humph,

It's been a long time since I've written, I'm afraid, but having recently been seeing Sir Ralph Cochrane, Paul Brickhill, Mick and a few others re the 617 history, I thought it was the moment to get in touch with you.

Cochrane has been trying to organise an official story of 617 for a long time and having considered various possible authors has finally settled on Brickhill. Chiefly for the reasons that he is an established author and that he is an ExRAF operational pilot. The whole thing is being done officially and on a high level and Sir Ralph has asked me to contact the Squadron with a view to getting their help. You of course are a pretty key person as far as supplying gen goes.

I gather that you have had in mind the idea of writing a book yourself and that although you haven't actually done so you have kept a fairly copious diary. None of us knew this of course and therefore I can see that the situation is a little difficult. I am afraid that the sponsors of the 617 history wouldn't accept your book, assuming that you propose to write it, as the official version because you are not a pilot and because it would be your first book. At the same time they actually don't want to do anything to interfere with your private plans. You can well imagine, however, how keen we all are that Brickhill's book should be as complete as possible and it obviously won't be quite the same without your diary being available to him.

My object in writing to you is to ask whether you can suggest any arrangement whereby Brickhill could have access to this diary, or failing that to have your views on the subject. I am writing in the name of the Squadron and with the purpose of ensuring that the history shall be as full as possible.

All the very best, *as ever*
Leonard Cheshire

I could never refuse him anything and so I agreed and there then followed much correspondence with Brickhill. Throughout the period of this correspondence – with Cheshire, Brickhill and subsequently with the film company who made the film – there were always comments to the effect that there was room for my own personal reminiscences.

At the beginning of 1954 I had my first communication from Associated British Picture Corporation Ltd at Elstree. It said,

14 January 1954

Dear Mr Humphries

We have for some time been making preparation for a film of the magnificent operation carried out in 1943 by 617 Squadron, Royal Air Force, in which the Moehne [sic] and Eder dams were destroyed, and which earned for them the title 'The Dam Busters'. Our film story, written by R. C. Sherriff, is based mainly on Paul Brickhill's book of the same name, but we have also received considerable information, encouragement and assistance from the Air Ministry, Mr Barnes Wallis, Air Chief Marshal Sir Ralph Cochrane, Group Captain Whitworth, Wing Commander H. B. (Micky) Martin and many others closely connected with the events portrayed, all of whom have now read our script and expressed their approval.

In endeavouring to tell the whole story from the time the idea was first conceived until it was so successfully carried out we are very conscious of the fact that it has not been possible to pay full credit to everyone concerned for their part in this great achievement, but have necessarily had to concentrate on a selected group of characters. You will see, however, there are a number of scenes in which the Adjutant of 617 squadron (referred to as S. D. O. in the script) participates. As you were at this time holding this appointment we would be glad if you would kindly read the script and let us know that the scenes, as written, have your approval.

We should, at the same time, be very interested to have any other comments which you might like to make.

Yours sincerely,
W. A. Whittaker

I duly read the script, which I thought did justice to the squadron. I offered a few suggestions, pointed out a few minor errors and omissions, corrected some procedural matters and gave then a few insights into the men, such as the rather interesting fact that 'Dinghy' Young was quite interested in Yoga and used to spend much of his time during beer drinking sessions sitting cross legged on tables with a tankard in his hand

In the film, my part was limited to a few scenes of door openings and the like.

The first concrete contribution I actually made to perpetuate the tribute to 617 was the production of a scrapbook of original memorabilia and the presentation of it to Grantham Museum. Time and again I read over my story and though I contributed a number of articles to various magazines over the years I felt that the story had been quite fully told and whilst I was sorry that I had not published my own story, as I have said before, I had my memories

However some of the more recent tales and publications I felt bordered on fantasy. Some contained what I considered to be untruths and I very much felt that I should complete what I had started all those years ago to set the record straight.

Report from the *New York Herald Tribune*

Wing Commander Guy P. Gibson, VC, DSO and Bar, DFC and bar, hero of the smashing of the Möhne and Eder dams last summer, spoke recently to the Herald Tribune public forum on current affairs:

It is a great honour and a great privilege to be here tonight, talking to you in New York City, on the last few days that I will be in this country. I have been down to Florida, up north to Chicago, Detroit and out west to Hollywood, where I had a very good time, and everywhere I have found the most charming people in the world.

But I might say that you are probably all wondering why we are so young. Well I might tell you that in England the Eighth Air Force and ourselves have placards put up in every bar that all lieutenants colonel under the age of 19 must be accompanied by their parents when they go into a bar. But I, ladies and gentlemen, am here to speak to you as a bomber pilot, in a very limited time, and I'd like to tell you what we feel over there in England bombing the Germans.

Our idea is not to bomb Germany out of the war by bombing alone (although if we could do it it would be a very nice little gift and a way to shorten the war): what we are trying to do is soften her up to such a tune that when we do invade France, as we surely will, then we will have a punch-drunk enemy. This in turn will save lives, save lives of our young men, your young men, young men who are going to plan the future of this world: young men who I hope, when they come home will be able to have a free life and will be able to live free for the rest of their lives.

I might say that these aerial battles which we fight on their account involve often 6,000 or 8,000 young men, and the strain is tremendous. Picture the scene. Picture England in autumn. The leaves are falling, the grass is still green, everything is very pretty. A crowd of young men may be playing games, they may be playing a ball-game, they may be riding, they might be taking their girls out to a movie show, they might be doing anything – and then suddenly throughout the villages and the towns, loudspeakers blare. 'All crews report back to your bases immediately!' A few swift hours later those boys are 600 miles from home, fighting for their lives above a German Target, whether it is day or night.

I might say these night raids and day raids which I have been in are, in a way, the most thrilling things, and in another way the most gruesome. You are talking to your pals, boys you were brought up with, and then suddenly you see one of them burn up, and down he goes, and you know you've got one pal less.

I hate the Germans for that reason. I hate them for many things but I hate them for this reason. I started this war in a squadron which bombed Kiel Canal on September 3, 1939. I started the war with 25 chaps, four great friends of mine. I knew their sisters; we were brought up together. Now I am the last one left. That is why I hate the Germans, because I have lost all my friends.

Well, when we have bombed the Germans, we will turn our noses, our blunt bomber noses, toward Japan. I might tell you that there are many ways of conquering Japan. Bombing is one of them. A combination of bombing and sea power is another, but as I am just a bomber pilot I'll be proud to lead the first British air fleet over Tokyo itself, and I'll be proud to drop the first 2,000-pounder on the emperor's palace.

I'm leaving America in a few days' time. As I said, I've never had such a good time for a long time as I've had over here. And I hope after the war we'll see much more of each other, British and Americans. All I would like to say to you now, and it comes from the bottom of my heart, is when I go back to England I can tell all my boys, 'God bless America!'

Guy Gibson, VC with his wife, Eve, after the investiture

Citation

The citation for Wing Commander Guy Gibson's VC.

From the *LONDON GAZETTE* – 28 May 1943

Acting Wing Commander Guy Penrose Gibson, DSO, DFC, Reserve of Air Force Officers, No 617 Squadron

This officer served as a night bomber pilot at the beginning of the war and quickly established a reputation as an outstanding operational pilot. In addition to taking the fullest possible share in all normal operations he made single handed attacks during his 'rest' nights on such highly defended objectives as the German battleship *TIRPITZ*, then completing in WILHELMSHAVEN.

When his tour of operational duty was concluded, he asked for a further operational posting and went to a night-fighter unit instead of being posted for instructional duties. In the course of his second tour, he destroyed at least three enemy bombers and contributed much to the raising and development of new night fighter formations.

After a short period in a training unit he again volunteered for operational duties and returned to night bombers. Both as an operational pilot and as a leader of his squadron, he achieved outstandingly successful results and his personal courage knew no bounds. BERLIN, COLOGNE, DANZIG, GYDNIA, GENOA, Le CRUESOT, MILAN, NUREMBURG and STUTTGART were among the targets he attacked by day and by night.

On conclusion of his third operational tour, Wing Commander GIBSON pressed strongly to be allowed to remain on operations and he was selected to command a squadron then forming for special tasks. Under his inspiring leadership, this squadron has now executed one of the most devastating attacks of the war – the breaching of the MOHNE and EDER dams.

The task was fraught with danger and difficulty. Wing Commander GIBSON personally made the initial attack on the MOHNE dam. Descending to within a few feet of the water and taking the full brunt of the anti-aircraft defences he delivered his attack with great accuracy. Afterwards he circled very low for thirty minutes drawing the enemy fire on himself in order to leave as free a run as possible for the following aircraft which were attacking the dam in turn.

Wing Commander GIBSON then led the remainder of his force to the EDER DAM where, with complete disregard for his own safety he repeated his tactics and once more drew on himself the enemy firing so that the attack would be successfully developed.

Wing Commander GIBSON has completed 170 sorties involving more than 600 hours operational flying. Throughout his operational career, prolonged exceptionally at his own request, he has shown leadership, determination and valour of the highest order.

R.I.P.

Final Resting Places of the 'Dam Raid' Aircrew

Wing Commander G. P. GIBSON, VC, DSO, DFC
Steenbergen-en-Kruisland RC Cemetery, NL

Sgt Byers. Harlingen Cemetery, NL.
FltLt Astell. Reichswald War Cemetery, Cleve.
FltLt Barlow. Reichswald War Cemetery, Cleve.
FltLt Hopgood. Reinburg War Cemetery, north of Krefield.
PO Burpee. Bergen – op – Zoom Cemetery, NL.
PO Ottley. Reichswald War Cemetery, Cleve.
SqnLdr Maudsley. Reichswald War Cemetery, Cleve.
SqnLdr Young. Bergen General Cemetery, NL.

The above were the pilots of the aircraft so I assume crewmembers were buried in the same cemetery.

Guy Gibson's grave at Steenbergen

[114]

Roll of Honour 1943–1945

In my office we had a crewboard with their photographs arranged in rows, starting with the pilot, then flight engineer, followed by air bomber, navigator, wireless operator and the two gunners. When an aircraft was reported missing, they were taken down from the board and retained until definite information, usually from the International Red Cross, was received advising us of the fate of the airmen.

I decided to keep the details in a rough squadron diary I had started and, as and when we received information, I wrote this up. I do not have photographs of all the men on the Roll of Honour, nor do I have all their details but what I do have is recorded here. The two pages of photographs will give you an idea of what I kept. The other pages of photographs were too poor to be reproduced but the entries I made against those names are shown in full.

Most of the photographs had only the surname of the man on the back but, in most cases, I was able to match them to a pilot, date of action, and the target. I did not think then that 60 years later I would be reproducing them.

The entries are a bit 'rough-and-ready' but it is right that they should be shown here as a reminder that these very young men made it possible for others to live their lives.

D. Allatson
KIA September 1943. Dortmund Ems Canal.
R. A. P. Allsebrook, DSO, DFC
KIA 16th September 1943. Dortmund Ems Canal.
C. T. Anderson
S. R. Anderson, DFM
J. L. Arthur (Can)
W. Astel,l DFC
KIA 16th May 1943. Dambuster.
R. N. G. Barlow, DFC (Aust)
KIA 16th May 1943. Dambuster.

E. A. Barnett

J. K. Barrett, DFC
    Navigator. KIA 16th May 1943. Dambuster.

G Bell

A. W. Benting
    KIA 16th September 1943. Dortmund Ems Canal.

W. D. Bickle

E. C. A. Blake
    KIA 16th September 1943. Dortmund Ems Canal.

R. Bolitho
    KIA 16th May 1943. Dambuster.

N. A. Botting, DFC
    KIA 16th September 1943. Dortmund Ems Canal.

J. G. Brady (Can)

C. Brennan
    KIA 16th May 1943. Dambuster.

A. W. Buck

S. Burns
    KIA 21st December 1943. Liege. Dambuster.

P. S. Burgess
    KIA 16th May 1943. Dambuster.

L. J. Burpee, DFM (Can)
    Pilot Officer KIA 16th May 1943. Dambuster.

N. R. Burrows
    KIA 16th May 1943. Dambuster.

V. W. Byers (Can)
    KIA 16th May 1943. Dambuster.

G. E. Cansell
    KIA 8th October 1944. Kembs Barrage.

H. G. Clarke

M. T. Clarke, DFC

G. H. Coles (Can)
    KIA 16th September 1943. Dortmund Ems Canal.

A. P. Cottam (Can)
    Wireless operator. KIA 16th May 1943. Dambuster.

R Cummings (USA)
    KIA 10th December 1943 during special operation in occupied territory.

N. J. Davidson (Can)

G. A. Deering, DFC (Can)
> Air Gunner. KIA 16th September 1943. Dortmund Ems Canal. Dambuster.

J. McB. Dempster, DFM (Can)

W. G. Divall
> KIA 16th September 1943. Dortmund Ems Canal.

W. A. Duffy, DFC (Can)
> Pilot. Killed on active service 7th August 1944. Crashed Mosquito on Wainfleet bombing range.

K. Earnshaw (Can)

J. A. Edward, DFC
> Flight Lieutenant. KIA 24th June 1944. Wizernes.

M Ellwood, DFM

E. Ewan

H. W. Felton, DFM

R. Florence, DFM (NZ)
> KIA 17th November 1943. Failed to return from Africa.

J. Fort, DFC
> KIA 15th September 1943. Crashed into sea after aborted raid.

C. L. Fox
> Killed on active service 16th September 1944. Missing on return from *Tirpitz* raid.

M. J. D. Fuller

F. A. Garbas (Can)
> KIA 16th May 1943. Dambuster.

A. Garshowitz (Can)
> KIA 16th May 1943. Dambuster

G. P. Gibson, VC, DSO, DFC

K. Gill, DFC, C de G

A. Gillespie, DFM
> Air bomber. KIA 16th May 1943. Dambuster.

H. S. Glinz (Can)
> KIA 16th May 1943. Dambuster.

J. I. Gordon, DFC (Aust)

C. B. Gowrie (Can)

C. F. M. Graham
> KIA 16th September 1943. Dortmund Ems Canal.

J. M. Grant, DFC
KIA 16th May 1943. Dambuster.

G. H. Green

G. H. F. G. Gregory, DFM
Flying officer. KIA 16th May 1943. Dambuster.

L. D. Griffiths

W. C. Grimes, DFM

P. W. Groom
Flight Engineer. Killed on active service 16th September 1944. Missing on return from *Tirpitz* raid.

B. A. Gumbley, DFM (NZ)

J. Guterman, DFM
KIA 16th May 1943. Dambuster.

S. G. Hall (Aust)

G. J. Harden, DFC

E. A. Hartley
KIA 8th October 1944. Kembs Barrage.

W. Hatton
Killed on active service 15th September 1943. Crashed into sea after aborted raid.

F. C. Hawkins
KIA 8th October 1944. Kembs Barrage.

R. C. Hay, DFC (Aust)

A. L. Hath

K. A. J. Hewitt

V. Hill

S. Hitchen
KIA 16th September 1943. Dortmund Ems Canal.

G. W. Holding, SDO, DFC

A. D. Holding

A. A. Holt
KIA 31st July 1944. Rilly le Montagne.

H. W. Honig
KIA 8th October 1944. Kembs Barrage.

J. V. Hopgood, DFC
KIA 16th May 1943. Dambuster.

D. Hopkinson
KIA 16th May 1943. Dambuster.

E. Hornby
    KIA 16th September 1943. Dortmund Ems Canal.
T. Horrocks
    KIA. No other details.
D. T. Horsfall
    Flight Engineer. KIA 16th May 1943. Dambuster.
B. J. Hosie (NZ)
    KIA 8th October 1944. Kembs Barrage.
C. J. G. Howard
    Flight Lieutenant. KIA 8th October 1944. Kembs Barrage.
R.G . Howell
    KIA possibly 10th December 1943, on secret operation in occupied
    territory.
T. J. Hurdiss
    KIA 8th October 1944. Kembs Barrage.
R. E. G. Hutchinson, DFC
J. W. Hutton
W. Ibbotson
    Air Gunner KIA 16th May 1943. Dambuster.
P. Ingleby
    Killed on active service. Crashed Mosquito 7th August 1944 on Wainfleet
    bombing range.
S. Isherwood
    KIA 26th June 1944. Wizernes.
B. Jagger, DFM
C. McA. Jarvie
T. Jaye
J. I. Johnson, DFC (Can)
T. W. Johnson
    KIA 16th September 1943. Dortmund Ems Canal.
T. B. Johnston
    KIA 16th May 1943. Dambuster.
I. G. Jones
R. N. Jones
P. Kely, DFC
G. A. Kendrick
L. W. J. King, DFC

J. Kinnear
Flight Engineer. KIA 16th May 1943. Dambuster.

L. G. Knight, DSO (Aust)
KIA 16th September 1943. Stayed with aircraft while crew baled out. Dortmund Ems Canal. Dambuster.

W. Knight

C. M. Knox

A. McN. Laughland, DFM (Can)
Killed on active service 1th7 November 1943. Failed to return from Africa.

F. Levy (Rhodesia)
Pilot. Killed on active service 16th September 1944. Missing on return from *Tirpitz* raid.

J. R. G. Liddell

T. W. Lloyd, DSO

W. C. A. Long

R. D. Lucan, DFM
KIA 8th October 1944. Kembs Barrage.

R. B. S. Lulham
KIA 16th September 1943. Dortmund Ems Canal.

V. S. MacCausland (Can)
KIA 16th May 1943. Dambuster.

R. McFarlane

R. C. MacArthur
KIA 15th September 1943. Dortmund Ems Canal.

J. McDowell (Can)

G. M. McGuire
Wireless operator. Killed on active service 16th September 1944. Missing on return from *Tirpitz* raid.

A. F. McKeller

A. F. McNally (Can)
Killed on active service. 16th September 1944. Missing on return from *Tirpitz* raid.

D. J. H. Maltby, DSO, DFC
Squadron leader. Killed on active service 15th September 1943. Crashed into sea returning from aborted raid on Dortmund Ems Canal. Dambuster.

J. Marriott (Can)
Flight Engineer. KIA 16th May 1943. Dambuster.

R. Marsden
    KIA 16th May 1943. Dambuster.
H. E. Maudsley, DFC
    KIA 16th May 1943. Dambuster.
T. W. Maynard
    KIA 2st1 December 1943. Liege.
T. A. Meikle, DFM
L. Mieyette (Can)
    KIA 16th September 1943. Dortmund Ems Canal.
G. S. Miles
J. W. Minchin
    KIA 16th May 1943. Dambuster.
P. Moore
    KIA 16th September 1943. Dortmund Ems Canal.
J. F. Naylor
L. W. Nichols
    Wireless operator. KIA 16th May 1943. Dambuster.
V. Nicholson, DFM
    Killed on active service 15th September 1943. Crashed returning from aborted
    operation.
J. P. Nugent
B. J. de C. O'Grady (Can)
    Killed on active service 17th November 1943. Aircraft failed to return from Africa.
T. V. O'Shaughnessy
    Flight Lieutenant. Killed on active service 21st January 1944. Crashed on
    flying exercise.
W. Ottley, DFC
    KIA 16th May 1943. Dambuster.
R. C. Paterson
T. H. Payne
    KIA 16th September 1943. Dortmund Ems Canal.
E. E. S. Peck
    Air bomber. Killed on active service 16th September 1944. Missing on return
    from *Tirpitz* raid.
G. Pegler
J. O. Peltier (Can)
    KIA 31 July 1944. Rilly le Montagne.

C. P. Pesme (Can)
    KIA. No other details
L. Plishka (Can)
R. H. Pool
    KIA 5th August 1944. Wizernes.
D. J. D. Powell
J. L. Powel,l DFC
T. W. P. Price
H. J. Pringle, DFC
J. Pulford, DFM
    Flight Engineer. KIA 13th February 1944. Crashed on return to base. Dambuster.
J. C. Randon
A. W. Richardson
J. P. Riches
C. W. Roberts
B. Robinson
    Believed KIA 10th December 1943.
J. A. Rodger
    KIA 16th September 1943. Dortmund Ems Canal.
J. G. Rolton, DFC
    KIA 31st July 1944. Rilly le Montagne.
I. S. Ross (Aust)
D. C. Shea DFC
    Killed on active service 16th September 1944. Missing on return from *Tirpitz* raid.
H. T. Simmonds
    KIA 14th September 1943. Crashed on return from aborted raid. Dambuster.
J. S. Simpson
    KIA 16th September 1943. Dortmund Ems Canal.
E. C. Smith
    KIA 20th December 1943. Liege.
F. M. Spafford, DFC, DFM (Aust)
D. G. W. Stewart
J. McL. Stewart
A. J. Stone
    Wireless operator. Killed on active service 14th September 1943. Crashed into sea on returning from aborted raid on Dortmund Ems Canal. Dambuster.

G. S. Stout, DFC
> Flying Officer. KIA 23rd September 1943. Dortmund Ems Canal.

H. J. Strange
> Rear Gunner. KIA 2st1 December 1943. Liege. Dambuster.

W. R. Suggest, DFC (Can)

H. T. Tearoom, DFC (Can)
> Navigator. KIA with SqdLdr Holden, 16th September 1943. Dortmund Ems Cana.l Dambuster.

T. J. Tate
> Flight Lieutenant. KIA 8th October 1944. Kembs Barrage.

A. J. Taylor
> KIA 16th May 1943. Dambuster.

D. G. Thomas
> Gunner. Killed on active service 16th September 1944. Missing on return from *Tirpitz* raid.

D. M. Thorpe (Can)

J. W. Thrasher (Can)
> KIA 2st1 December 1943. Liege.

E. G. Tilby

R. D. Trevor-Roper, DFC, DFM

W. J. Tytherleigh, DFC
> KIA 16th May 1943. Dambuster.

R. A. Urquhart, DFC (Can)
> KIA 16th May 1943. Dambuster.

W. N. Wait
> KIA 5th August 1944. Wizernes.

A. J. Walker, DFC

W. Walker

W. Walter
> KIA 10th December 1943 during special operation in occupied territory.

E. J. Walters (USA)

J. H. Warner
> Navigator. KIA 16th May 1943. Dambuster.

D. W. Warwick (Can)
> KIA 16th September 1943. Dortmund Ems Canal.

D. T. Watkins, DFC
> KIA. No other details.

J Watson

G. H. Weedon (Can)
>   Flying officer. KIA 19th December 1943 during special operation in occupied territory.

J. L. Welsh, DFM

R. Welsh

L. G. Weller

S. L. Whillis
>   Flight Engineer. KIA 16th May 1943. Dambuster.

A. N. Whitaker

S. J. Whittingham, DFM

F. A. Wile (Can)
>   KIA 16th May 1943. Dambuster.

J. Wilkinson

A. A. Williams

C. R. Williams, DFC (Aus)
>   KIA 16th May 1943. Dambuster.

R. H. Williams, DFC

H. S. Wilson
>   KIA 16th September 1943. Dortmund Ems Canal.

P. E. Woods
>   KIA 8th October 1944. Kembs Barrage.

D. R. C. Wyness, DFC

R. B. Yates

G. A. Yeo
>   KIA 16th May 1943. Dambuster.

H. M. Young, DFC (USA)

E. E. G. Youseman, DFC

THE SURVIVORS

DORTMUND EMS CANAL RAID – 16th September 1943.
FO Stout's plane was shot down.
Reg Petch
>   Escaped and returned to England.

Rupert
>Escaped and returned to England.

FO Knight's plane was shot down.

F. E. Sutherland
>Sergeant. Escaped and returned to England. Dambuster.

E. C. Johnson
>Escaped and returned to England. Dambuster.

R. E. Grayston.
>Flight Engineer. Captured and imprisoned in a POW camp. Dambuster.

Sidney Hobday
>Navigator. Escaped and returned to England. Dambuster.

H. E. Obrien
>Gunner. Captured and imprisoned in a POW camp. Dambuster.

DAM RAID – 16th May 1943

FltLt Hopgood's plane was shot down.

H. F. G. Frazer, DFM
>Pilot Officer, captured and imprisoned in a POW camp. Dambuster.

Anthony F. Burcher, DFM, RAAF
>Pilot Officer, captured and imprisoned in a POW camp. Dambuster.

PO Ottley's plane was shot down before reaching target. Freddie Tees was the only survivor. Dambuster.

TIRPITZ RAID – October 1944

On the return from the *Tirpitz* raid one plane crashed in Sweden.

Willy Carey (Aust), the flying officer was injured in the crash but returned to the UK along with Gerry Witherick, Flight Engineer Franks and McKie, the navigator.

RILLY LE MONTAGNE RAID – 31st July, 1944

Flight Lieutenant Reid, VC and Luker were shot down and imprisoned in a POW camp.

BREST RAID – 5th August 1944

Flying Officer Cheney (Can) was shot down over target but evaded capture and returned to England along with Curtis and Roshner. McRostie was captured and imprisoned in a POW camp.

WIZERNES RAID – 24th June 1944

Flight Lieutenant Edwards was shot down and imprisoned in a POW camp.

Rice

> Flying Officer. Shot down on Liege raid and imprisoned in a POW camp.

McLennan

> No information.

Flight Sergeant Young

> No information.

Sharpe

> No information.

Hewstone

> No information.

Buntain

> No information.

Beasley

> No information.

McDonald

> No information.

Identity Card Photographs.

S/LT
Humphries
ADJ 617.

F/O TAERUM
R.C.A.F.
Gibsons Nav

P/O Deering
Gibsons
(Gunner)

SGT PULFORD
GIBSONS
FL/ENGINEER.

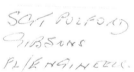

DAVE SHANNON
PILOT
Dam Raid.

Bill JOHNSON
Pilot
Dam Raid.

DIED OF
WOUNDS
BERGEN.

ROLL of HONOR.

F/O KENDRICK

Roll of
Honour

SGT ROBINSON

SGT HOWELL
Roll of Honour

Killed on Active
Service.
Special
Target
France

P/O Norden

Roll of
Honour

Roll of
Honour . P/O PLISHKA

SGT BAXTERS.

Roll of
Honour.

Roll of
Honour.

F/Sgt. Whittingham.
DFM

Roll of
Honour

F/Sgt GRIMES
DFM

Roll of
Honour

F/Sgt Jagger
DFM

Roll of
Honour.

F/Sgt CUMMINGS

A Sort of Epilogue

To those who have been interested in my efforts to present a story of the 'Dambusters' squadron, please spare a thought for the elderly gentleman who had to motivate himself to finish a task he started over fifty years ago. The spark, which I suppose was always there, was fanned into a flame after it was brought to my attention that one of the last publications on this history of the 617 was so outrageously a hideous untruth that it was an insult to anyone, living or dead, connected with the Dambusters.

I have earlier vaguely referred to those who have climbed on the back of the fame of Guy Gibson and his successors but that effort made me so angry that I felt it was time for someone who was there for the birth of 617 Squadron in the spring of 1943, and the following two years, to tell the story.

I have also felt that, in my writings all those years ago, I did not really give the very deserved accolades to Wing Commander Cheshire and Wing Commander Tait, our second VC and quadruple DSO respectively. They led from the front throughout, flying Lancasters, Mosquitos and the Mustang, achieving, with their crews, a level in bombing accuracy that enabled them to take out strictly military targets, which contributed greatly to the eventual defeat of Germany.

The Barnes Wallis 'Tallboy' and later the amazing 'Grand Slam' bomb destroyed submarine pens, bridges and many underground bunkers thought to be impregnable. The 'Tallboy' was the bomb which eventually led to the destruction of the *Tirpitz*, the attacks being led by Willie Tait. The battleship was finally despatched in November 1944 as it lay moored in Tromsø fjord. I have a recollection of attending a film on this raid, presumably recorded by our photographic aircraft.

It has to be remembered that although the Squadron achieved its fame after the epic Dam raids there are 203 names on the Roll of Honour. I lived with them from formation to nearly the end of the war, and each and every one of them had the same level of courage and dedication as the 'originals'. I have to believe that men of their calibre are still entering the RAF. I hope so.